MAKING A
MINIATURE HOUSE

GUY R. WILLIAMS
With diagrams by the author

London
OXFORD UNIVERSITY PRESS
1964

Oxford University Press, Amen House, London E.C.4

GLASGOW NEW YORK TORONTO MELBOURNE WELLINGTON
BOMBAY CALCUTTA MADRAS KARACHI LAHORE DACCA
CAPE TOWN SALISBURY NAIROBI IBADAN ACCRA
KUALA LUMPUR HONG KONG

Author's thanks are due to many friends for help and advice in the preparation of this book. He is especially grateful to Mr. Richard Claughton, Mr. Adrian Gibson, and Ian Stoner for their invaluable assistance.

Printed in Great Britain by
W. & J. Mackay & Co. Ltd., Chatham, Kent

CONTENTS

200100

1 Planning

Model houses exercise a great fascination, even on people who have long ago ceased to play with toys. This book shows that you can make a delightful, true-to-scale miniature house without expensive equipment, and without preliminary training. If you follow the simple directions given, you will have, when you have finished, something that is more than a toy, something that is rather like a miniature work of art.

THE BASIC MATERIALS AND THE TOOLS
(Other optional materials are specified in the text, as required)

You will be able to build your miniature house in quite a short time if you can appoint some definite area to be your workshop where you can keep your tools, accessories, materials, plans, and half-finished components. You will not need much space for your 'workshop' as the house will be only 36 in. long by 20 in. wide when you have finished it.

Your working surface should be firm and flat. A carpenter's bench would be ideal, but most household tables will also be strong enough to support the comparatively light equipment and to stand up to the strains.

A table with a polished surface, or any other surface that may be easily damaged, should be covered with a thick blanket or some other adequate form of protection. A sheet of newspaper is not enough—it will absorb paint and other liquids, and, besides, it may tear.

Woods (see diagram 1): Plywood: For the walls, floors, ceilings and roof.
Blockboard: Although you will find plywood the most convenient material to use, you may choose blockboard for the thicker end walls and the base.
Stripwood: For the furniture. You can buy it in such sections as $\frac{1}{16} \times \frac{1}{8}$ in., $\frac{1}{16} \times \frac{1}{4}$ in., $\frac{1}{8} \times \frac{1}{8}$ in., and $\frac{1}{8} \times \frac{1}{4}$ in.

[1]

Block-board

Ply-wood

THE BASIC MATERIALS AND THE TOOLS

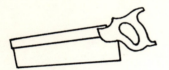

[2a] Tenon-saw

Tools (see diagrams 2a–2f): Tenon-saw or panel-saw for cutting plywood. A panel-saw is a crosscut saw with very fine teeth.

G-cramp to hold the wood down to the working surface while it is cut.

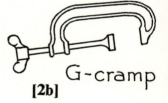

G-cramp

[2b]

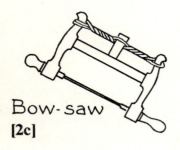

Bow-saw

[2c]

Bow-saw or fret-saw to cut out doors and windows (optional).

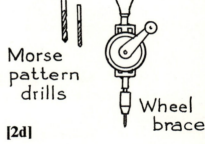

Morse pattern drills

Wheel brace

Wheel brace with a small selection of Morse pattern drills.

[2d]

Firmer chisel

[2e]

Chisel with a blade about ¾ in. wide for 'chopping out'.
Steel plane or jack-plane for finishing the outside edges of the components (optional).
Surform file or plane for smoothing rough edges. You may, however, use glass-paper instead, Middle 2-Grade and Grade No. 1.
Hammer, pliers, bradawls, nails or panel pins (optional).

Glue: You may use Scotch glue or other traditional material, but modern synthetic glues such as 'Aerolite' and 'Casco Glue-All' are perfectly suitable, or one of the excellent impact or contact glues, such as 'Evo-stik'.

Additional Material: Pencil HB or H. Marking-knife or pen-knife. Rule with a straight edge. Pair of compasses. Set-square or carpenter's try-square. Ruling pen (optional). Soft indiarubber.

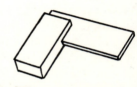

[2f] Try-square

HOW TO SHARPEN A PLANE BLADE AND A CHISEL

For sharpening edged tools you will need an oilstone and a piece of leather, glued to a piece of wood, to act as a strop.

The Plane Blade: To remove the cutting iron from a metal plane you have to release the lever cap.

To remove the cutting iron from a wooden jack-plane or trying-plane, strike the front of the plane lightly to release the wedge and keep the back end of the plane against your thigh to provide the necessary pivoting movement.

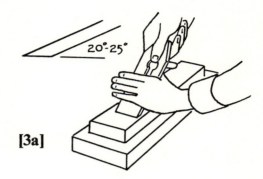

[3a]

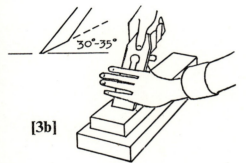

[3b]

When sharpening the iron, hold it with its bevel flat against the oilstone (see diagram 3a), raise the end slightly (see diagram 3b) and work it backwards and forwards. If you give a little extra pressure with your right and your left hand alternately, you will give a slight curve to the iron which is desirable (see diagram 3c).

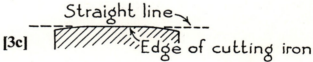

[3c]

Make sure from time to time that there are no gaps or gashes. If you are using the oilstone correctly, you should eventually raise a distinct burr or 'wire edge' along the cutting edge. When you have done this, put the iron flat side down on the oilstone (see diagram 4) and move it backwards and forwards once or twice. This will turn the wire edge to the bevel side of the iron. Then turn the iron over again and repeat the process until the wire edge breaks away.

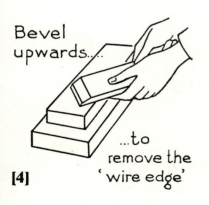

[4]

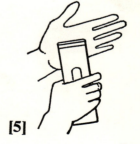

[5]

With a leather strap or the palm of your hand you can put a final polish or keenness on the cutting edge (see diagram 5).

HOW TO SHARPEN A PLANE BLADE AND A CHISEL

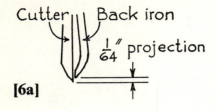

[6a]

When you replace the cutter and back iron in the plane, make sure that the leading edge of the back iron is only $\frac{1}{64}$ in. away from the cutting edge of the cutter (see diagram 6a). Then put the back iron and the cutter in the body of the plane so that the cutter projects only a little below the sole of the plane (see diagram 6b).

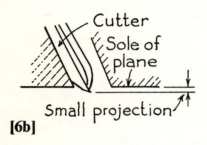

[6b]

Diagram 7 shows how you should hold a plane when finishing a plywood edge. Grip the handle with your right hand, making sure that your forefinger rests on the end of the cutter. With the finger-tips of your left hand help to control the direction when moving the plane.

[7]

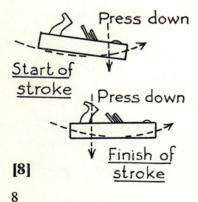

[8]

Diagram 8 shows how to apply pressure to a plane—at the front of the tool with your left hand at the beginning of each stroke; at the back of the tool with your right hand at the end of each stroke.

When using a plane you should put the plywood in a vice to make sure that it does not shift about. If you have only a metal vice, line the jaws with strips of straw-board or cardboard to prevent any damage to the plywood. Work from the corner of the wood towards the centre to achieve the wanted dimension.

The Chisel: A chisel has two bevels, a 'grinding bevel' at an angle of 20 or 25 deg., which is already on the chisel when you buy it, and a 'sharpening bevel', which you will have to make yourself (see diagram 9).

First put the chisel with the grinding bevel flat on the oilstone (see diagram 10). Then lift the chisel up to an angle of 30 or 35 deg. and move it backwards and forwards until the cutting edge shows a small burr or 'wire edge'. Remove this by putting the chisel flat on the oilstone with the bevelled side upwards and moving the tool gently backwards and forwards. Then finish by stropping the cutting edge gently on a piece of leather.

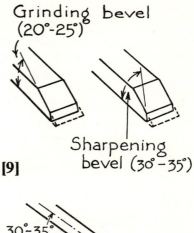

Grinding bevel (20°-25°)

Sharpening bevel (30°-35°)

[9]

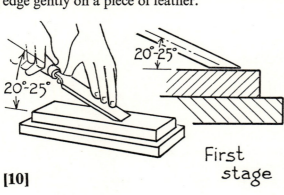

20°-25°

20°-25°

First stage

[10]

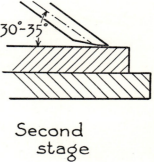

30°-35°

Second stage

WORKING TO SCALE

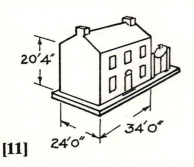

20'4"

34'0"

24'0"

[11]

All models should be made to a definite scale to look convincing. The miniature house described in this book has been planned to a scale of one-sixteenth full size—that is to say, ¾ in. of model represents 1 ft. of actual house. Diagram 11 shows the life-size measurements that will be represented by the model.

Before you start work, mark off a strip of card or thin wood with your scale which you may like to use to convert small-scale measurements into life-size as you are making the miniature house. Mark off a number of ¾ in. divisions along one edge (see diagram 12a) and divide the first length into four equal parts, each of which will represent 3 in. (see diagram 12b).

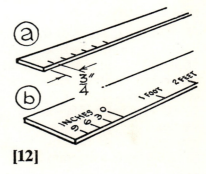

ⓐ

ⓑ

¾"

1 FOOT   2 FEET

INCHES 9 6 3 0

[12]

2 Base, Walls and Roof

THE BASE

The foundation of the miniature house must be firm and flat. Take a piece of $\frac{1}{2}$ in. thick plywood or blockboard and make it to the dimensions shown in diagram 13, but be careful that each corner is exactly 90 deg. The safest procedure to achieve exact corners is outlined below:

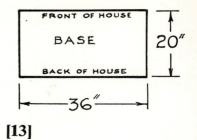

[13]

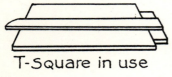

T-Square in use

[14] Try-Square

(1) Make one of the long edges as straight as you can.

(2) Using that edge as a 'datum' or starting point, mark off two perpendicular lines exactly 36 in. apart with a T-square or a try-square (see diagram 14). Draw the lines first with a sharp pencil, then scribe along them with a marking-knife or penknife (see diagram 15). Keep your forefinger on top of the blade, as you do when holding a pen, and use a metal straight edge for guiding the knife. If you want your work to be especially well finished, draw and scribe all marking-out lines on the reverse side of the wood as well as on the top surface.

[15]

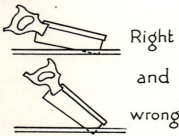

Right

and

wrong

ways of sawing

[16] plywood

(3) Saw along the lines you have drawn, keeping the cut well to the waste side, so that there is a gap of at least $\frac{1}{16}$ in. between the saw-blade and the line. Hold the saw at an acute angle (see diagram 16). Any saw held at an incorrect angle will tend to tear plywood, though the knife-cuts used before for marking will help to minimize this effect.

(4) Remove the surplus wood from the waste side of both lines, using a metal plane or jack-plane, or a Surform file or plane. You may also use a file or a piece of glass-paper, held over a small wooden block, but working with these is comparatively slow.

   If you use a file instead of a plane to remove the surplus wood, put the board in a vice, with a strong, thick piece of wood on each side to support the plywood and to guide the file (see diagram 17).

Pieces of wood to guide and support

File

Plywood

[17]

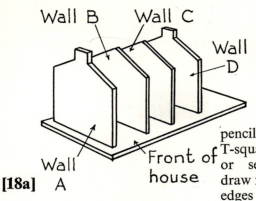

Wall B   Wall C

Wall D

Front of house

[18a]   Wall A

When you have finished the two short sides of the base, mark out the remaining side, 'rough-cut' and finish it in the way just described, and then mark out the positions for the walls (see diagrams 18a–f).

Take a sharp pencil, a rule and a T-square, try-square or set-square, and draw first the outside edges of the outside walls, as shown with dotted lines in diagram 18b.

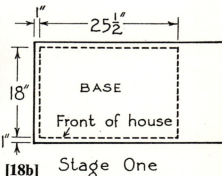

BASE

Front of house

[18b]   Stage One

Next, draw the lines that represent the inside edges of the outside walls A and D. These are shown with full lines in diagram 18c.

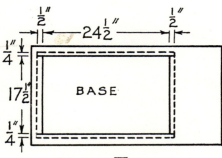

BASE

[18c]   Stage Two

After that draw the centre lines of the two side-facing interior walls B and C, as shown with chain-dot lines in diagram 18d. Note that the first dimension (9 in.) is measured from the dotted line you have drawn at Stage One.

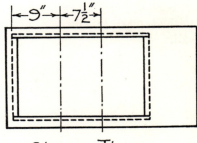

[18d] Stage Three

Finally, add the lines representing the edges of Walls B and C. As these walls will be made from $\frac{1}{4}$ in. thick plywood, each line will have to fall $\frac{1}{8}$ in. away from one of the centre lines and parallel to it (see diagram 18e).

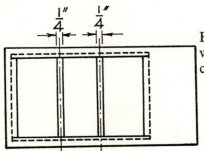

[18e]   Stage Four

Check the accuracy of the dimensions, and then shade the areas for the side-facing walls to mark their position clearly (see diagram 18f).

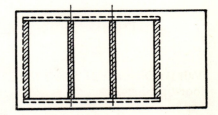

[18f] Stage Five

THE WALLS

The Side-Facing Walls A, B, C and D: Next, draw and cut out the side-facing walls. Wall A and Wall D, which are outside walls, are made from $\frac{1}{2}$ in. thick plywood, the interior walls B and C are made from $\frac{1}{4}$ in. thick plywood.

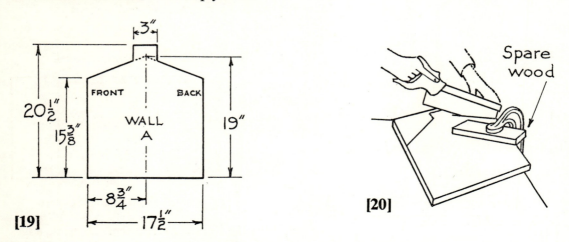

[19]

[20]

Wall A: The outside shape of Wall A is shown in diagram 19. When you saw the roof-slope, hold the plywood down on your working surface with a G-cramp, putting a piece of wood between the pressure surface of the cramp and the plywood (see diagram 20). When you have finished, mark this piece of wood as 'Wall A' and also mark on it the front and the back of the wall.

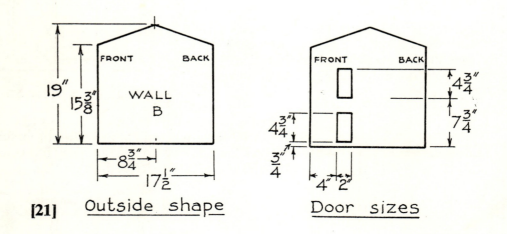

[21]   Outside shape   Door sizes

Wall B: Diagram 21 shows the outside shape of Wall B and the position and shape of the two door-openings.

After you have drawn out the door-openings in Walls A and B on both sides of the wood, scribe along the marked lines with a sharp knife.

12

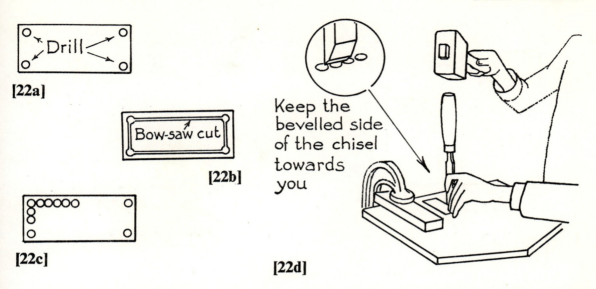

[22a]

[22b]

[22c]

[22d]

To cut out the door-openings, first put a large, flat piece of wood under the plywood piece so that you can drill through without damaging the table. Then drill a hole near each of the four corners of the door-opening (see diagram 22a). After that rough-cut from hole to hole with a fret-saw or bow-saw (see diagram 22b). If you have no suitable saw you may drill a number of holes that are almost touching (see diagram 22c) and break down the connecting pieces with a sharp chisel. Then slice out the rest of the waste wood with a chisel (see diagram 22d). If you have a wooden mallet you can use it to provide the downward pressure.

Work back by a series of steps, finishing on the scribed line. Do not cut right through the wood but let the chisel blade travel about half-way through the thickness. Then turn the wood over and complete the cut from the reverse side. When you cut, be careful that the edges of the door-openings are perfectly straight and at right angles to the larger surface of the wall.

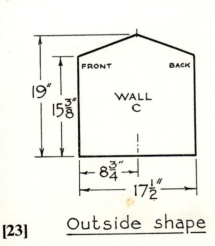

Outside shape

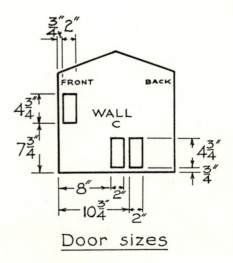

Door sizes

[23]

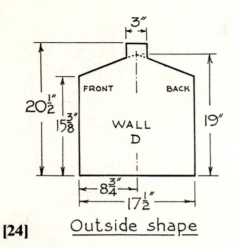

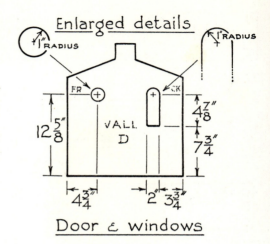

Enlarged details

[24] Outside shape

Door & windows

Walls C and D: Their dimensions are shown in diagrams 23 and 24. Wall C is made from plywood $\frac{1}{4}$ in. thick and Wall D from plywood $\frac{1}{2}$ in. thick. Draw and cut these walls out as accurately as you have drawn and cut out Walls A and B, using the same techniques. Then write 'Front of House' and 'Back of House' on each wall in the appropriate places.

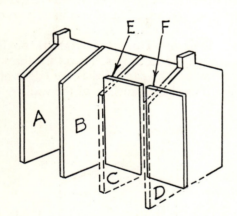

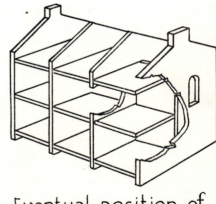

Eventual position of interior
[25] front-facing walls (E & F)

Eventual position of
floors and ceilings

Before you leave Walls A, B, C and D, mark on the indoor surfaces the positions of the floors, ceilings, and interior front-facing walls E and F (see diagrams 25 and 26). Then shade the areas between the sides of Walls E and F and between the top and the bottom edges of the floors and ceilings (see diagram 26).

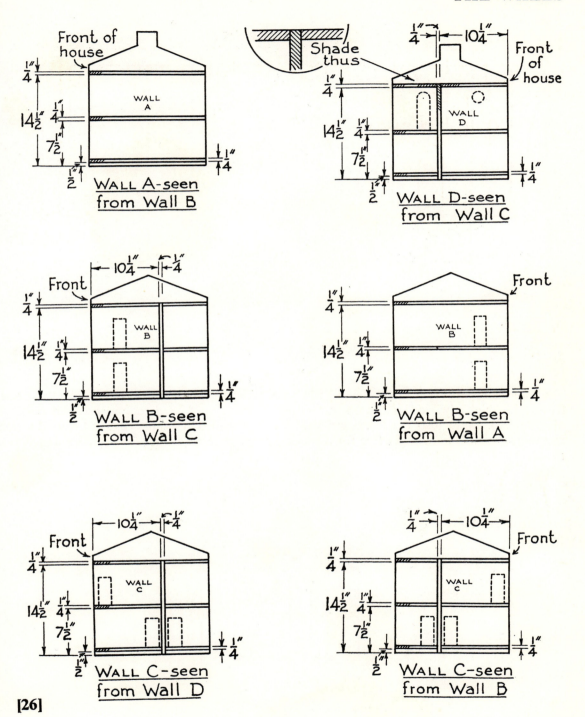

Shade thus

WALL A-seen from Wall B

WALL D-seen from Wall C

WALL B-seen from Wall C

WALL B-seen from Wall A

WALL C-seen from Wall D

WALL C-seen from Wall B

[26]

THE WALLS

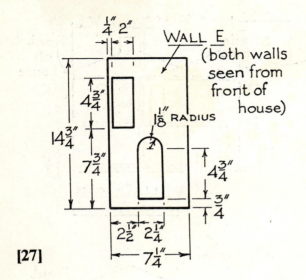

WALL E
(both walls seen from front of house)

$\frac{1}{4}$" 2"

$4\frac{3}{4}$"

$14\frac{3}{4}$"

$7\frac{3}{4}$"

$1\frac{1}{8}$" RADIUS

$4\frac{3}{4}$"

$\frac{3}{4}$"

$2\frac{1}{2}$" $2\frac{1}{4}$"

$7\frac{1}{4}$"

[27]

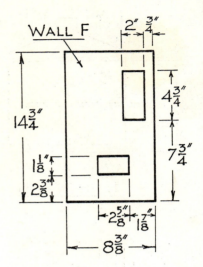

WALL F

2" $\frac{3}{4}$"

$14\frac{3}{4}$"

$4\frac{3}{4}$"

$7\frac{3}{4}$"

$1\frac{1}{8}$"

$2\frac{3}{8}$"

$2\frac{5}{8}$" $\frac{7}{8}$"

$8\frac{3}{8}$"

The Interior Front-facing Walls E and F: For the dimensions see diagram 27. Make these walls from $\frac{1}{4}$ in. thick plywood and mark the positions of the floors and ceilings on both sides (see diagram 28). Mark also the front and back of each wall. On Wall F cut out also the small rectangle which later will provide for a serving hatch in the wall between kitchen and dining-room.

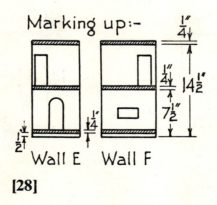

Marking up:-

$\frac{1}{4}$"

$\frac{1}{4}$"

$14\frac{1}{2}$"

$7\frac{1}{2}$"

$\frac{1}{4}$"

$\frac{1}{2}$"

Wall E   Wall F

[28]

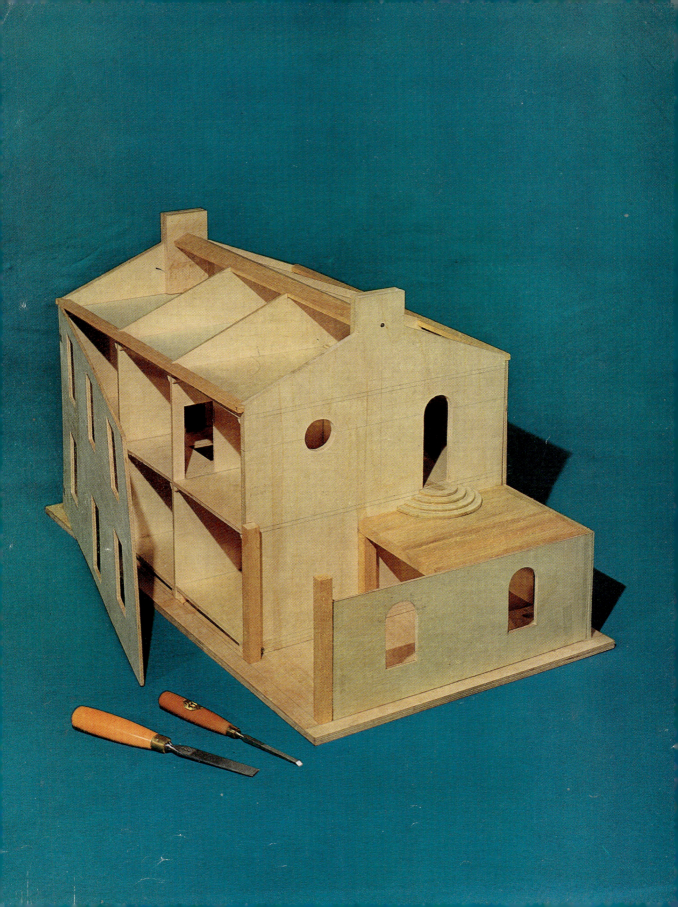

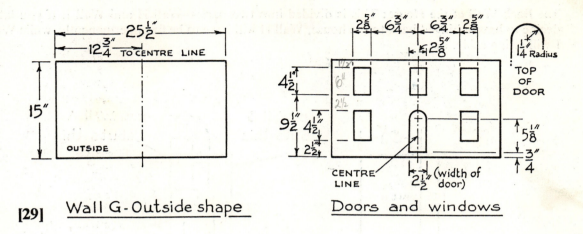

[29] Wall G - Outside shape

Doors and windows

The Front of the House, Wall G: The dimensions of the front of the house (Wall G) are given in diagram 29. Use ¼ in. thick plywood for this wall and draw and cut it out as you have done with the other walls. Then mark it with 'Outside of House' and 'Inside of House', and on the inside surface mark the positions of the side-facing walls, floors and ceilings (see diagram 30). Eventually, Wall G may either be made completely removable, or hinged to the finished house as shown in the colour plate facing page 16.

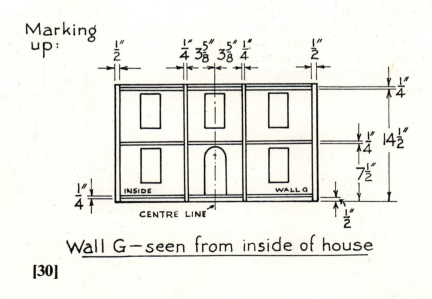

Wall G — seen from inside of house

[30]

THE WALLS

The Back Wall of the House: This is divided into two parts—Wall H and Wall I. If you later decide to have a hinged back to the house, Wall H will have to be fixed permanently, while Wall I will swing aside.

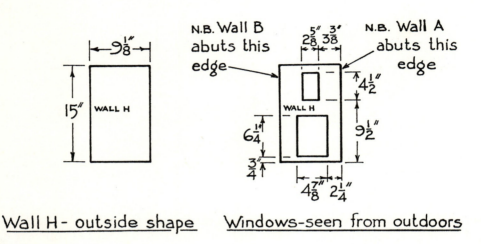

Wall H - outside shape   Windows-seen from outdoors

[31]

Wall H: This is made from $\frac{1}{4}$ in. thick plywood. For the outside shape, dimensions and the sizes and positions of the windows see diagram 31. Mark the front and the back of the wall, and on the front-facing surface mark the positions of the floors and ceilings (see diagram 32).

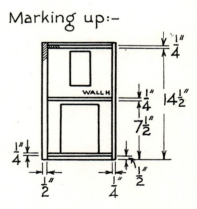

Marking up:-

Wall H - seen from inside of house

[32]

18

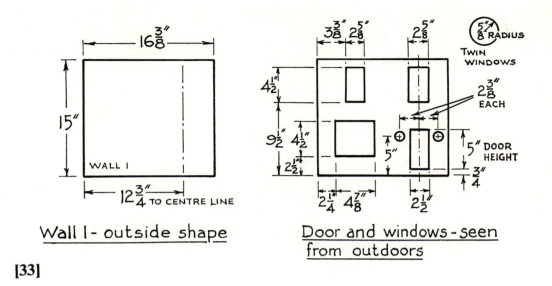

Wall I - outside shape

Door and windows - seen from outdoors

[33]

Wall I: This, too, is made from ¼ in. thick plywood, and the outside shape, dimensions, sizes and positions of the windows are shown in diagram 33. Mark the front and back surfaces and the floor and ceiling levels as before (see diagram 34).

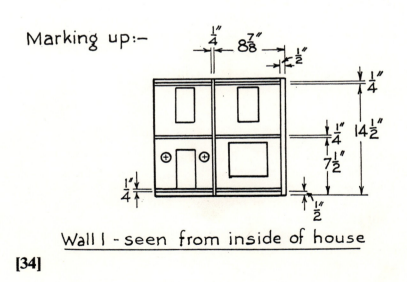

Marking up:—

Wall I - seen from inside of house

[34]

ADDING SUPPORTS FOR WALLS AND FLOORS

Before assembling the walls to the base you should add wooden supports, or locating strips, to each of them.

First, glue to the base six locating strips, made from $\frac{1}{2} \times \frac{1}{2}$ in. wood, in the following lengths: two are $17\frac{1}{2}$ in. long, two $10\frac{1}{4}$ in., and two 7 in. (see diagram 35).

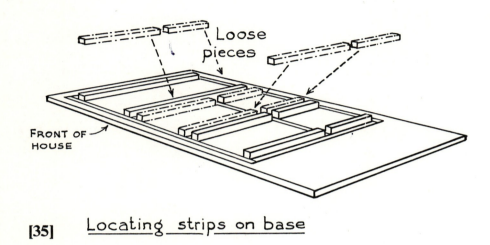

Loose pieces

FRONT OF HOUSE

[35]   Locating strips on base

At the same time you can prepare four more strips from $\frac{1}{2} \times \frac{1}{2}$ in. wood: two are $10\frac{1}{4}$ in. and two are 7 in. long. These strips are shown with dotted lines in diagram 35, but they will not be glued to the base until the final assembly of the house.

Then take some $\frac{3}{8} \times \frac{3}{8}$ in. wooden quadrant—you can get this at most wood merchants' and handicraft shops—and cut it into the following lengths:

1 piece $3\frac{1}{2}$ in. long
8 pieces   7 in. long
5 pieces $7\frac{1}{4}$ in. long
1 piece $7\frac{3}{4}$ in. long
4 pieces $10\frac{1}{4}$ in. long
2 pieces $17\frac{1}{2}$ in. long

Glue these pieces to Walls A, B, C and D as shown in diagram 36, but remember that they will have to support the floors and ceilings, so their uppermost surfaces will have to be lined up exactly with the lower edges of these.

To apply pressure to the pieces of quadrant, while the adhesive dries, you can use small clamps, or small but heavy domestic appliances such as flat-irons, or fine panel pins.

In diagram 36 the dimensions are given also for the small removable block that is to support the front of the landing. Later, in diagram 55, you will see how to fix two $\frac{3}{16}$ in. diameter locating pegs in it. The holes for these pegs must be drilled in Wall B.

ADDING SUPPORTS FOR WALLS AND FLOORS

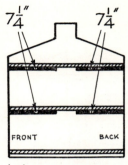

WALL A—seen
from Wall B

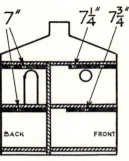

WALL D—seen
from Wall C

WALL C—seen
from Wall D

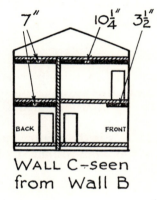

WALL C—seen
from Wall B

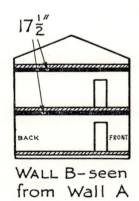

WALL B—seen
from Wall A

WALL B—seen
from Wall C

[36] Quadrant sizes, and positions

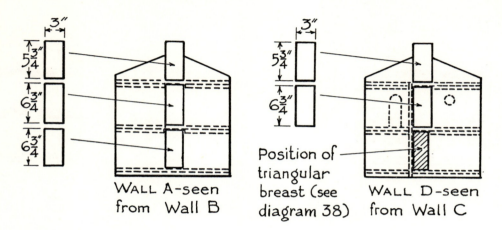

WALL A-seen from Wall B

Position of triangular breast (see diagram 38)

WALL D-seen from Wall C

[37]   Chimney breasts

Cut five flat pieces from ½ in. thick plywood (see diagram 37) and add them to the indoor surfaces of Walls A and D. The sixth piece is triangular in section (see diagram 38), and this should be glued to Wall D as shown with shaded lines in diagram 37.

Are you wondering why one part only of one of the chimney breasts is set at an angle of 45 deg. to the wall? This is the section that is to carry the dining-room fireplace, and it is set across the corner of the room so that any fire in the grate will warm the room as quickly and effectively as possible.

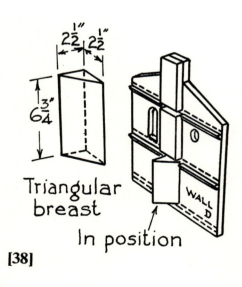

Triangular breast

In position

[38]

ASSEMBLING THE WALLS TEMPORARILY ON THE BASE

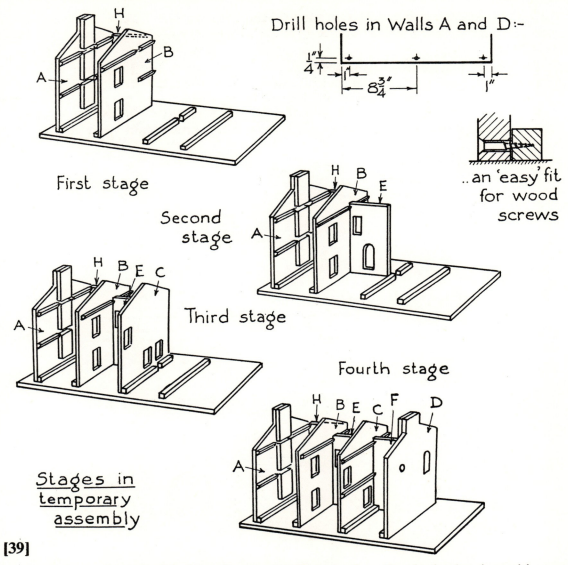

Drill holes in Walls A and D:-

..an 'easy' fit for wood screws

First stage

Second stage

Third stage

Fourth stage

Stages in temporary assembly

[39]

At this stage you may assemble the walls temporarily to see how they look when in position on the base. The easiest way to carry out the assembly is shown in diagram 39.

Place Walls A and B in their correct positions on the base. You may drill and countersink three small holes in Wall A (see top of diagram 39) to fasten its lower end temporarily with fine wood screws to the locating strip glued round the base.

Then place Wall H against the back ends of Walls A and B. Some strips of Sellotape will help to keep the walls together. Add Walls E and C as well as Walls F and D, fixing these in the same way, and finally put the front of the house (Wall G) and the movable back wall (Wall I) in position.

Now you will get a good idea of how the miniature house will look when it is complete.

THE ROOF RIDGE

The wooden member that will support the roof and keep Walls A, B, C and D at the correct distance from each other, is called the 'Roof Ridge'. There are two alternative ways of making a roof ridge:

(1) For a more difficult method you need a piece of wood, $23\frac{1}{2} \times 2 \times \frac{3}{4}$ in. Plane it carefully to the shape shown in diagram 40, and cut away recesses in Walls B and C to locate the ridge. If you drill holes on the vertical centre lines of Walls A and D, you can drive a countersunk head wood screw into each end of the roof ridge, which will enable you to fix the end walls at a constant distance from each other as well as providing a firm support for the roof.

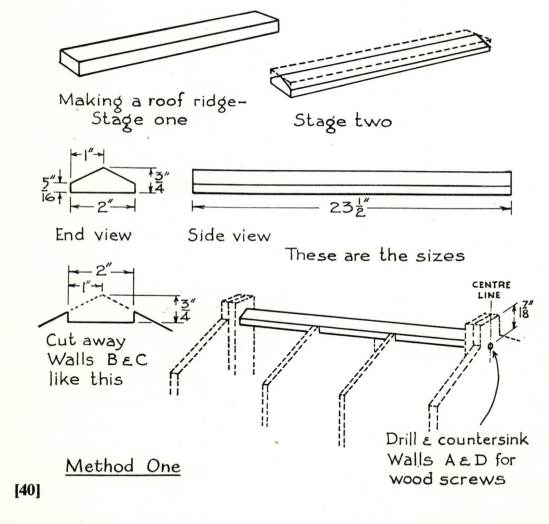

Making a roof ridge—
Stage one

Stage two

End view   Side view

These are the sizes

Cut away
Walls B & C
like this

Drill & countersink
Walls A & D for
wood screws

Method One

[40]

(2) Drill holes in Walls, A, B, C and D and place a piece of $\frac{5}{8}$ in. diameter dowelling, $25\frac{1}{2}$ in. long, through (see diagram 41). Later on, when you assemble the house finally, the locations will have to be made permanent with glue. This is the easier method of making a roof ridge.

24

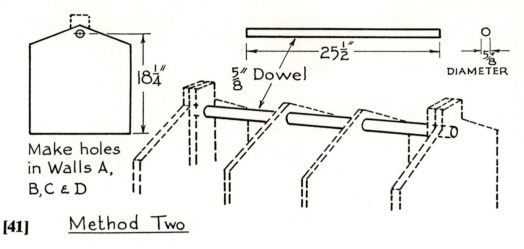

Make holes in Walls A, B, C & D

[41] Method Two

THE EAVES

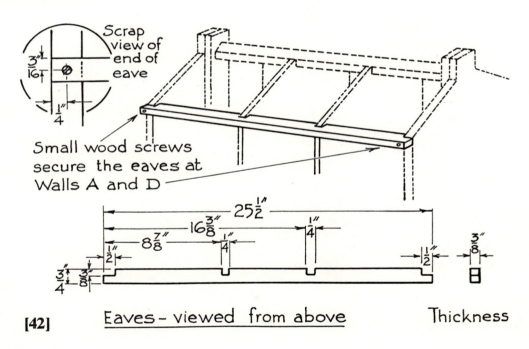

Scrap view of end of eave

Small wood screws secure the eaves at Walls A and D

[42] Eaves – viewed from above   Thickness

You will need two strips of wood to support the roof at the eaves. Make them from wood $25\frac{1}{2} \times \frac{3}{4} \times \frac{3}{8}$ in. and cut locating slots in one side of each eave. Make sure that these slots fit well on Walls A, B, C and D, and drill and countersink two holes in each piece. These holes are to take wood screws to secure the eaves to the sides of Walls A and D (see diagram 42).

25

THE ROOF

This is made from two pieces of $\frac{1}{4}$ in. thick plywood, each $25\frac{1}{2} \times 10\frac{1}{8}$ in. long (see diagram 43). Cut away two of the corners of each piece to clear the chimney stacks and chamfer the long edges with a plane or Surform tool so that they fit well together and rest nicely on the eaves (sectional drawing at the bottom of diagram 43). It is difficult to prescribe exact dimensions for these roof members as there will be almost certainly an infinitesimal difference between the sizes of any two assembled houses. So make the pieces a shade oversize at first and then trim the edges until the parts fit exactly.

Later, when the house has been finally assembled, you may glue some small blocks of wood to the under-surfaces of the two pieces of plywood that make the roof. Design and fit these 'locating blocks' so that the roof will readily slip back into its correct position if you have to remove it.

To represent slates or tiles, you can glue or paste corrugated cardboard to the roof, flattening the corrugations in a downward direction (see diagram 44).

You may also add tiling to the ridge by gluing together two lengths of $\frac{1}{4} \times \frac{1}{16}$ in. stripwood and one length of $\frac{1}{16}$ in. diameter dowel (see diagram 45).

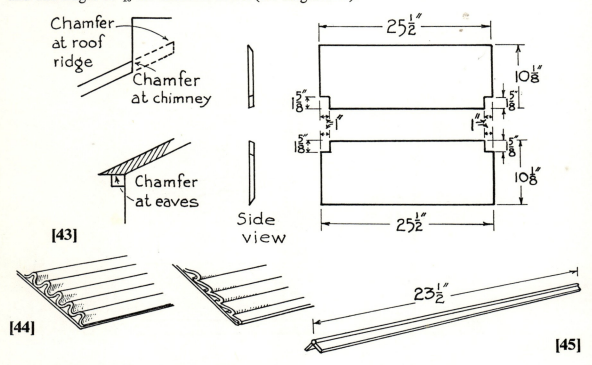

[43]   Side view

[44]   [45]

COLLECTING ODDS AND ENDS

Keep a look-out for small objects that are no longer needed and which may be easily converted into lighting fittings, paper racks, waste-paper baskets, and other details. For example, the newspaper tub in the sitting-room, which you can see in the foreground in the colour plate, facing page 32, is the inverted screw-on top of a whisky bottle. A collection of such oddments will give you plenty of material to choose from when you are working on the final stages of the house.

FLOORS AND CEILINGS

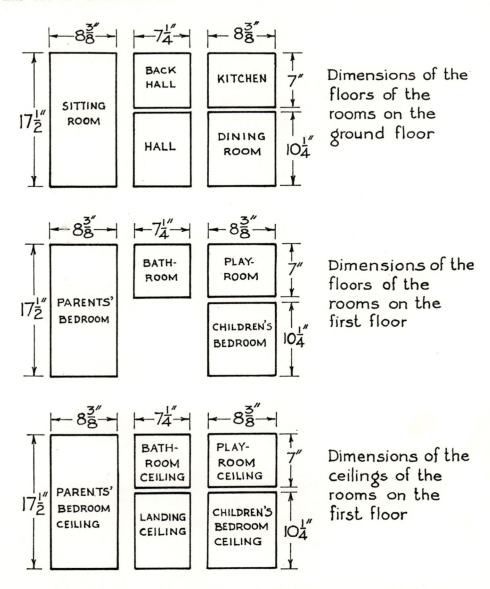

Dimensions of the floors of the rooms on the ground floor

Dimensions of the floors of the rooms on the first floor

Dimensions of the ceilings of the rooms on the first floor

[46]   Fourteen parts, to be made from plywood $\frac{1}{4}$" thick

As you cut out the fourteen pieces, which will represent the floors and ceilings, to the dimensions and shapes shown in diagram 46, try each in position in the house to make sure that it is an easy running fit. Finally label each piece clearly so as to show to which part of the house it belongs.

THE STAIRCASE

This has been designed as a single unit which incorporates a central passage-way with a curved ceiling, a cupboard, and a short side passage which will lead to the dining-room door. The unit will be built on the 'Hall Floor' so that later you can slide it in and out.

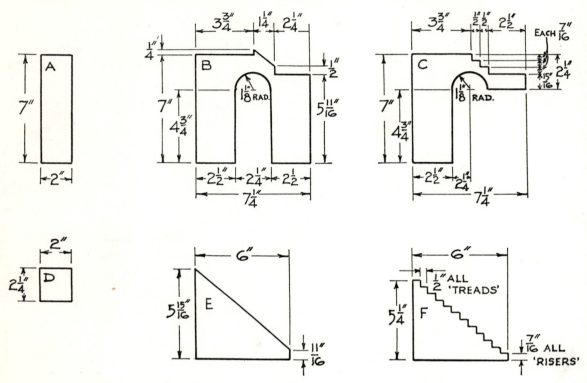

These six parts are made from plywood $\frac{1}{4}$" thick

[47]

Cut the parts of the staircase from plywood as shown in diagram 47 and clamp Pieces B and C together while you finish them so that the two semi-circular arches will match exactly.

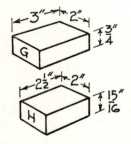

Diagram 48 shows two more substantial components which are cut from any suitable pieces of wood. Make sure that each is exactly 2 in. wide, or you will find it difficult to fix the stairs in position.

[48]

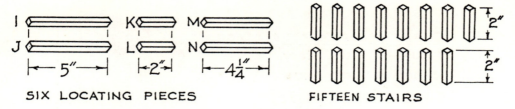

SIX LOCATING PIECES   FIFTEEN STAIRS

Parts of the staircase unit made from $\frac{1}{2}"x\frac{1}{2}"$ wood strip

[49]

The Stairs: Cut six locating pieces and fifteen stairs from wood strip to the lengths given in diagram 49, and label each piece with a letter.

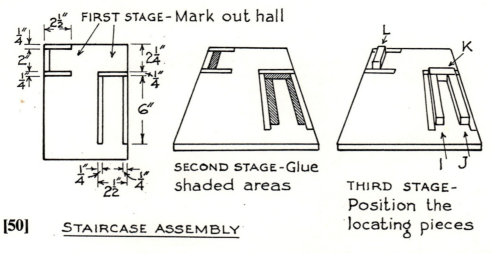

FIRST STAGE-Mark out hall

SECOND STAGE-Glue shaded areas

THIRD STAGE- Position the locating pieces

[50]   STAIRCASE ASSEMBLY

To Assemble the Staircase: Make a firm foundation by gluing the locating pieces I, J, K and L to the base (see diagram 50).

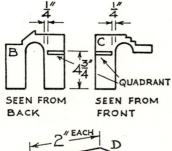

SEEN FROM BACK   SEEN FROM FRONT

QUADRANT

Fix the two lengths of quadrant that are to support the top of the cupboard (Piece D) in position on Pieces B and C (see diagram 51).

$\frac{3}{8}"x\frac{3}{8}"$ Quadrant

[51]

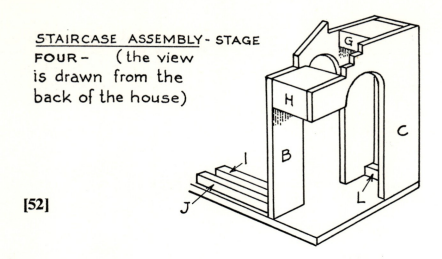

STAIRCASE ASSEMBLY - STAGE
FOUR – (the view
is drawn from the
back of the house)

[52]

Put Pieces A, B and C in position on the base and glue them together, with Pieces G and H in their correct positions (see diagram 52).

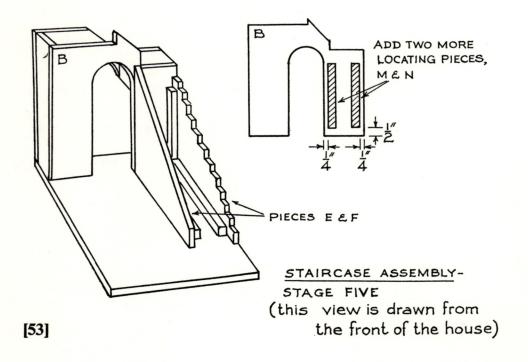

ADD TWO MORE
LOCATING PIECES,
M & N

PIECES E & F

STAIRCASE ASSEMBLY-
STAGE FIVE
(this view is drawn from
the front of the house)

[53]

When all the joints are dry, add the two locating pieces M and N to Piece B. When these are fixed firmly in position, add Pieces E and F (see diagram 53).

The Staircase Ceiling:

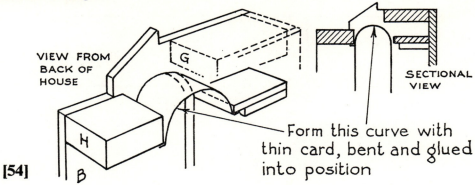

VIEW FROM
BACK OF
HOUSE

G

SECTIONAL
VIEW

H

[54]

B

Form this curve with
thin card, bent and glued
into position

Take a piece of thin white card or ivory board 3¾ × 2½ in., damp it with water, fasten it round a bottle with a diameter of approximately 2¼ in.—a standard half-pint milk bottle for example—and leave it to dry. When it is dry, glue it in position on Pieces B and C (see diagram 54).

Give the arch strength by coating the upper side (which will be hidden eventually) with Polyfilla or Alabastine, or with plaster of Paris mixed with cold water to the consistency of cream.

The shape and dimensions for a landing are given in diagram 55.

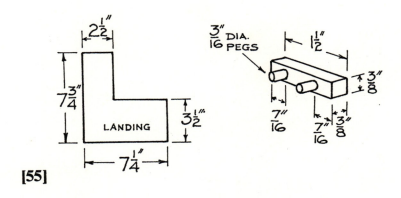

2½"

7¾"

LANDING

3½"

7¼"

[55]

$\frac{3}{16}$" DIA. PEGS

1½"

$\frac{3}{8}$"

$\frac{7}{16}$"

$\frac{7}{16}$"

$\frac{3}{8}$"

The Banisters: These can be made from transparent material, such as Perspex sheet 25 mm. thick which was used for the banisters shown in the colour plate facing page 17. If you have any difficulty in obtaining Perspex, write to Messrs. Imperial Chemical Industries Ltd., Imperial Chemical House, Millbank, S.W.1, and ask for your nearest retailer.

THE STAIRCASE

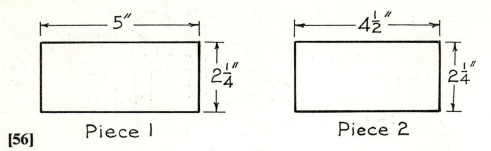

5″

$2\frac{1}{4}$″

Piece 1

$4\frac{1}{2}$″

$2\frac{1}{4}$″

Piece 2

[56]

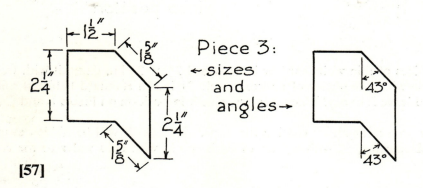

$1\frac{1}{2}$″

$1\frac{5}{8}$″

$2\frac{1}{4}$″

$2\frac{1}{4}$″

$1\frac{5}{8}$″

Piece 3:
← sizes
and
angles →

43°

43°

[57]

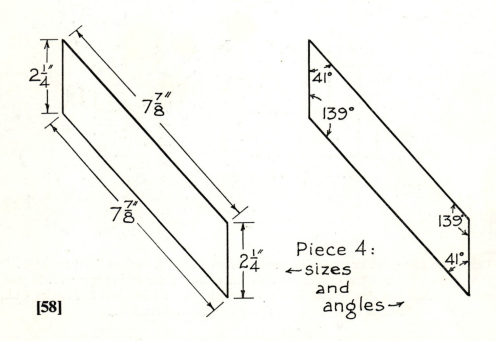

$2\frac{1}{4}$″

$7\frac{7}{8}$″

$7\frac{7}{8}$″

$2\frac{1}{4}$″

41°

139°

139°

41°

Piece 4:
← sizes
and
angles →

[58]

Draw the shapes (see diagrams 56, 57 and 58) first on a piece of stiff paper and cut them out to act as guides or templates. Perspex 25 mm. thick can be cut with a tenon-saw or a coping-saw, a hack-saw with a coarse blade, or one of the modern little wire-framed saws. Be careful not to scratch the smooth polished surface of the Perspex sheet.

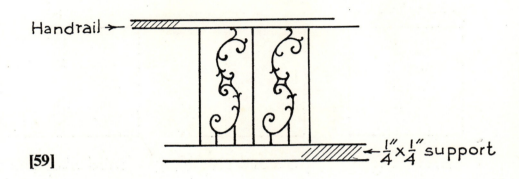

Handrail ➤

[59]

←¼″×¼″ support

The black wrought iron motif shown in diagram 59 can be repeated at regular intervals along the landing, or it can be slightly modified (see diagram 60) to suit the downward slope of the staircase.

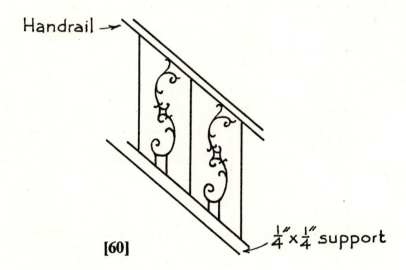

Handrail ➜

[60]

¼″×¼″ support

For drawing straight lines on Perspex use a ruling pen charged with Indian ink; for the curved lines you can use an ordinary pen. You can also take a very fine brush and 'blackboard black', obtainable at most ironmongers' and household stores.

Another method of drawing out the banisters is to make the design on white paper, to put this under the Perspex and to copy the lines through from the paper underneath.

THE CLOAKROOM

This is to be assembled on the piece of plywood marked 'Back Hall'.

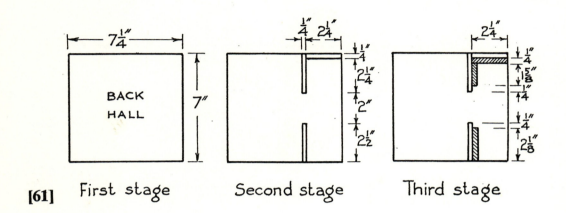

[61]   First stage   Second stage   Third stage

Mark up the plywood base (see diagram 61, Second stage) and glue to it three locating pieces cut from $\frac{1}{4} \times \frac{1}{4}$ in. wood strip (see diagram 61, Third stage).

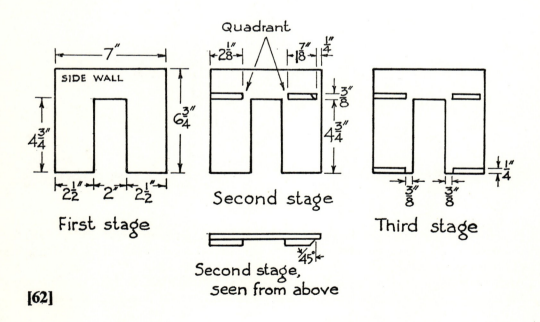

[62]

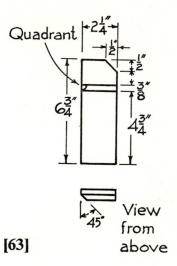

[63]

View
from
above

While the glue is drying, prepare from $\frac{1}{4}$ in. thick plywood the wall which is to contain the door (see diagram 62), and the smaller end wall (see diagram 63). To support the ceiling, glue pieces of $\frac{3}{8} \times \frac{3}{8}$ in. quadrant to both these walls.

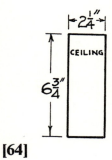

[64]

The ceiling should be cut from $\frac{1}{4}$ in. thick plywood (see diagram 64).

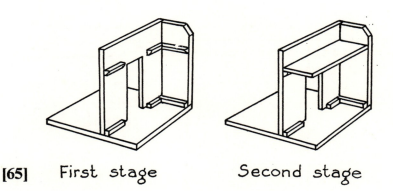

[65]   First stage   Second stage

Diagram 65 shows the assembly of the various main parts of the cloakroom. To cover the $\frac{1}{4} \times \frac{1}{4}$ in. skirting you may fit a 'false floor' made from cardboard or $\frac{1}{16}$ in. thick plywood, $\frac{1}{4}$ in. above the existing level, but if you do so you will have to add a step, $\frac{1}{4}$ in. high, at the door-opening.

THE GARAGE AND YARD

Walls and doors of the garage are made from plywood $\frac{1}{4}$ in. thick, the roof from wood $\frac{3}{4}$ in. thick. The gate piers, door piers and strengthening pieces are cut from wood $\frac{3}{4} \times \frac{3}{4}$ in., $\frac{3}{4} \times \frac{1}{2}$ in., and $\frac{1}{2} \times \frac{1}{2}$ in. Diagrams 66, 67 and 68 show the exact dimensions and the position of each part.

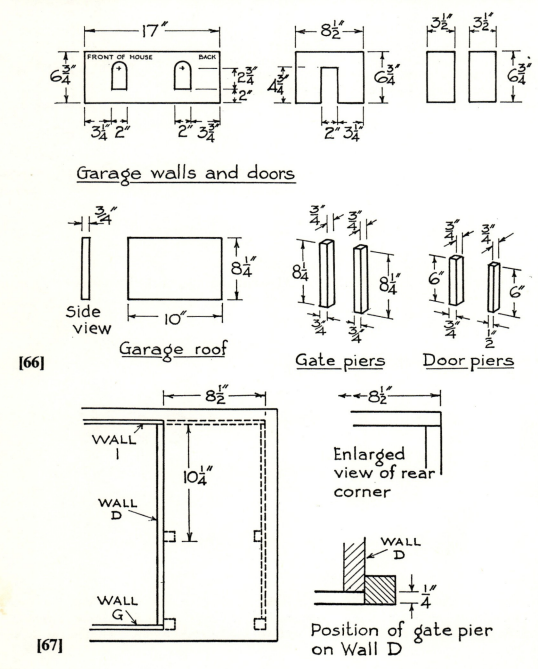

Garage walls and doors

Side view

Garage roof

Gate piers

Door piers

[66]

[67]

Enlarged view of rear corner

Position of gate pier on Wall D

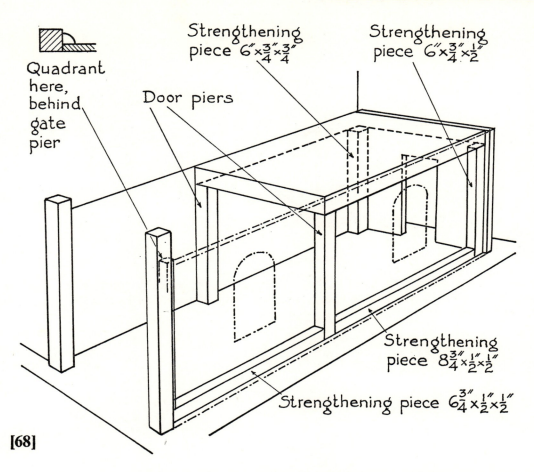

Quadrant here, behind gate pier

Door piers

Strengthening piece 6″×¾″×¾″

Strengthening piece 6″×¾″×½″

Strengthening piece 8¾″×½″×½″

Strengthening piece 6¾″×½″×½″

[68]

Extra strength can be given if holes are drilled through from the underside of the base so that fine countersunk head wood screws can be driven into the gate piers, door piers and upright strengthening pieces.

Instructions for making the little balustrade round the roof-garden are given in the following chapter.

4 Steps, Doors, Windows, and other Details

THE STEPS

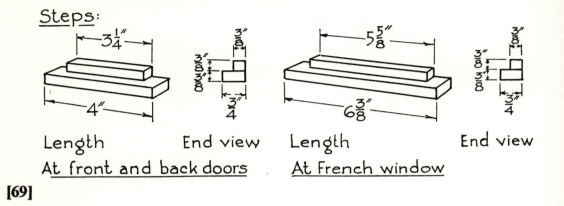

Steps:

Length
At front and back doors

End view

Length
At French window

End view

[69]

Shape and dimensions of the steps leading to the front door, back door and French windows are shown in diagram 69. Glue them to the front and back walls of the house, Walls G, H and I, in the appropriate positions.

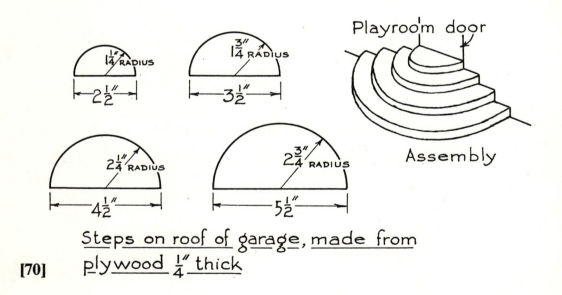

Steps on roof of garage, made from plywood $\frac{1}{4}''$ thick

[70]

The steps on the roof of the garage that lead up to the playroom door are shown in diagram 70.

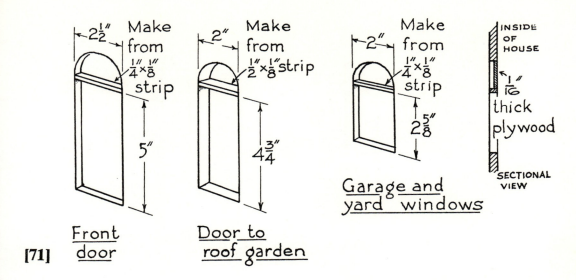

[71]

Front door

Door to roof garden

Garage and yard windows

Glue small lintels in the doorways in the front wall, Wall G, and the larger back wall, Wall I, as well as in the garage and yard windows (see diagram 71). The small sectional view in the right top corner of the diagram shows how to glue two semi-circular pieces of plywood above the lintels in the garage and yard windows so that the recesses formed echo the shapes of the windows in the end wall. When using plywood $\frac{1}{16}$ in. thick you may trim the pieces that are to fit in the recesses with a sharp pair of scissors.

The sizes of the doors are shown in diagram 72, and the dimensions of the framework are shown in diagram 73.

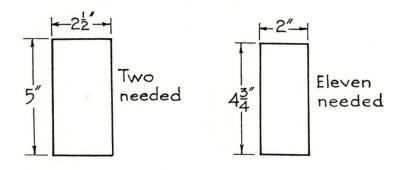

[72] Make all doors from plywood $\frac{1}{4}''$ thick

THE DOORS

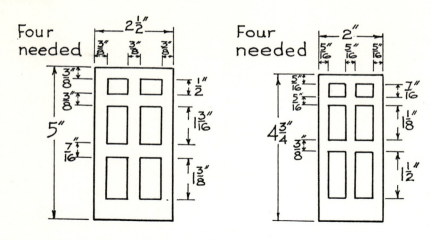

[73] Make these from plywood $\frac{1}{16}''$ thick

Only the front door and back door (see diagram 73, left) and the doors of the two reception rooms (see diagram 73, right) are panelled. All the other doors are left flush, but you may please yourself about the panelling.

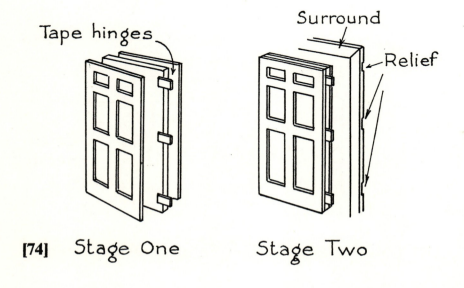

[74] Stage One   Stage Two

Cut the framework for the four panelled doors and fix metal or tape hinges in position before assembling the three constituent pieces (see diagram 74). Trim back all pieces of plywood and the surrounding mouldings so that the doors swing properly.

The Front Door:

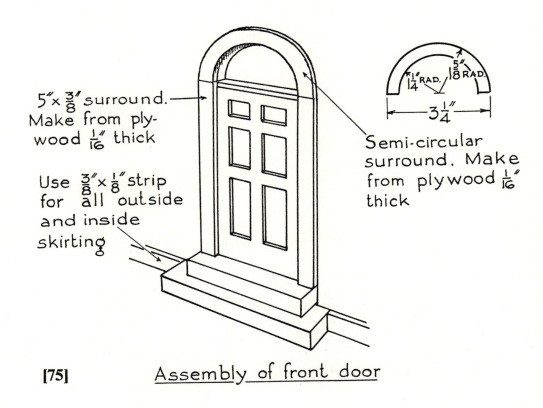

5″ x 3″ surround. Make from plywood 1/16″ thick

Use 3/8″ x 1/8″ strip for all outside and inside skirting

Semi-circular surround. Make from plywood 1/16″ thick

[75]

Assembly of front door

Diagram 75 shows the front door when it is nearly finished. You may add a knocker, letterbox, bell, and key plate before fixing the door in its final place. The semi-circular surround above the door can be cut with a sharp pair of scissors and finished with glass-paper.

THE DOORS

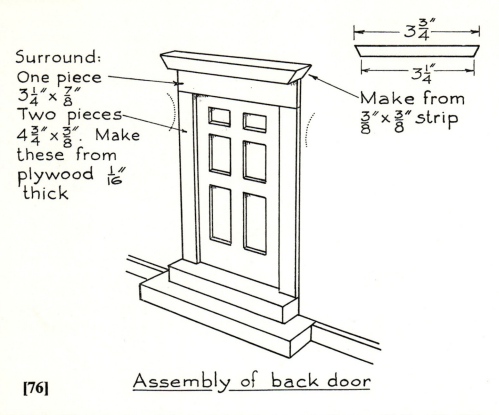

Surround:
One piece
$3\frac{1}{4}"\times\frac{7}{8}"$
Two pieces
$4\frac{3}{4}"\times\frac{3}{8}"$. Make
these from
plywood $\frac{1}{16}"$
thick

$3\frac{3}{4}"$

$3\frac{1}{4}"$

Make from
$\frac{3}{8}"\times\frac{3}{8}"$ strip

[76] Assembly of back door

The Back Door: The assembly of the back door is shown in diagram 76. To add a little variety, the appearance of the back door is slightly different from that of the front door. Before painting the house, initials, or the date, may be fixed above the door in raised letters.

To keep the sliding floors in place when the house is being moved, you may glue wooden strips round all the rooms, except the kitchen and bathroom, to act as skirtings. Use $\frac{3}{8}\times\frac{1}{8}$ in. or $\frac{3}{8}\times\frac{1}{16}$ in. strip, carry it round the doors (see diagram 77), and trim where necessary as shown in the drawings on the right of diagrams 74 and 77.

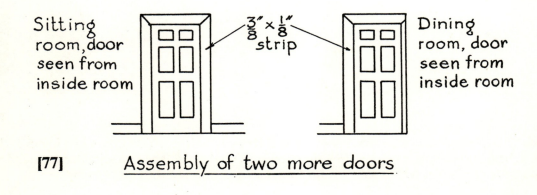

Sitting
room, door
seen from
inside room

$\frac{3}{8}"\times\frac{1}{8}"$
strip

Dining
room, door
seen from
inside room

[77] Assembly of two more doors

42

Cutting glass for windows as small as these is not easy. For the smaller windows use Acetate 15 mm. thick and for the larger windows thin Perspex. If you have any difficulty in obtaining Acetate, write to Messrs. Kettle, 127 High Holborn, W.C.1.

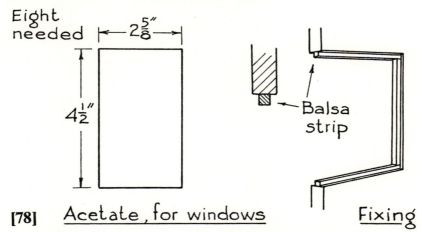

[78] Acetate, for windows   Fixing

To keep the rectangles of Acetate in place in the window apertures, use $\frac{3}{32} \times \frac{3}{32}$ in. balsa wood strip. Fix lengths of this with balsa cement along the narrow cut-out surfaces of the apertures, but make sure that the strip is placed centrally (see diagram 78).

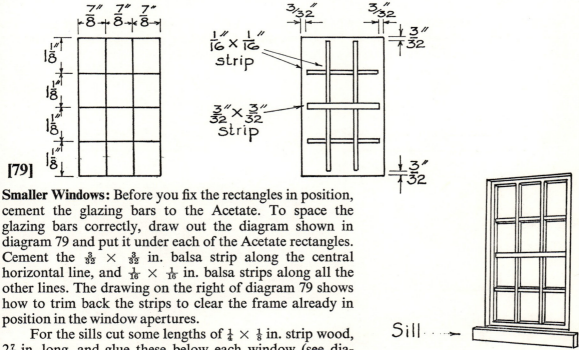

[79]

Smaller Windows: Before you fix the rectangles in position, cement the glazing bars to the Acetate. To space the glazing bars correctly, draw out the diagram shown in diagram 79 and put it under each of the Acetate rectangles. Cement the $\frac{3}{32} \times \frac{3}{32}$ in. balsa strip along the central horizontal line, and $\frac{1}{16} \times \frac{1}{16}$ in. balsa strips along all the other lines. The drawing on the right of diagram 79 shows how to trim back the strips to clear the frame already in position in the window apertures.

For the sills cut some lengths of $\frac{1}{4} \times \frac{1}{8}$ in. strip wood, $2\frac{7}{8}$ in. long, and glue these below each window (see diagram 80).

Sill

[80]   Window

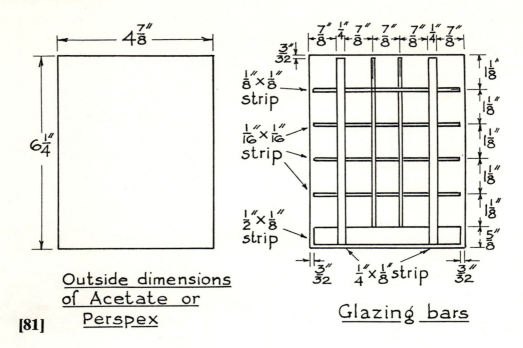

$4\frac{7}{8}''$

$6\frac{1}{4}''$

Outside dimensions
of Acetate or
Perspex

[81]

$\frac{7}{8}''$ $\frac{1}{4}''$ $\frac{7}{8}''$ $\frac{7}{8}''$ $\frac{7}{8}''$ $\frac{1}{4}''$ $\frac{7}{8}''$

$\frac{3}{32}''$

$\frac{1}{8}'' \times \frac{1}{8}''$ strip

$\frac{1}{16}'' \times \frac{1}{16}''$ strip

$\frac{1}{2}'' \times \frac{1}{8}''$ strip

$1\frac{1}{8}''$
$1\frac{1}{8}''$
$1\frac{1}{8}''$
$1\frac{1}{8}''$
$1\frac{5}{8}''$

$\frac{3}{32}''$ $\frac{1}{4}'' \times \frac{1}{8}''$ strip $\frac{3}{32}''$

Glazing bars

French Windows and Kitchen Window: Glaze these in the same way as the smaller windows. Diagram 81 shows how to cut out the French windows, the spacing of the glazing bars, and the kinds of strip to use. Diagram 82 gives corresponding details for the kitchen window.

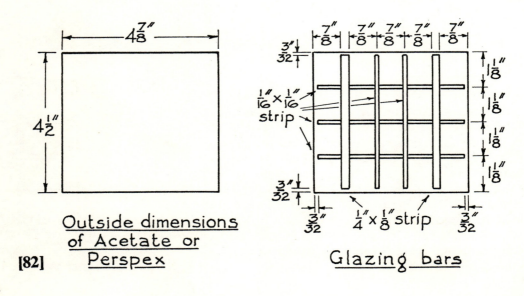

$4\frac{7}{8}''$

$4\frac{1}{2}''$

Outside dimensions
of Acetate or
Perspex

[82]

$\frac{7}{8}''$ $\frac{7}{8}''$ $\frac{7}{8}''$ $\frac{7}{8}''$ $\frac{7}{8}''$

$\frac{3}{32}''$

$\frac{1}{16}'' \times \frac{1}{16}''$ strip

$\frac{3}{32}''$

$1\frac{1}{8}''$
$1\frac{1}{8}''$
$1\frac{1}{8}''$
$1\frac{1}{8}''$

$\frac{3}{32}''$ $\frac{1}{4}'' \times \frac{1}{8}''$ strip $\frac{3}{32}''$

Glazing bars

The Fanlight: The fanlight over the front door will give you a chance to do an enjoyable bit of research, for you can see fine examples in almost every town and village in Britain. If you are unable to find one you like, use one of the designs shown in diagram 83.

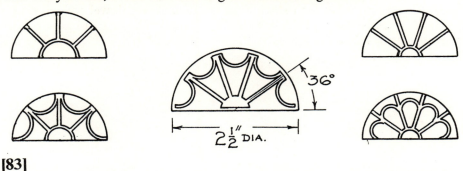

[83]

For the straight glazing bars cut some lengths from $\frac{1}{16} \times \frac{1}{16}$ in. balsa wood strip and cement these to the Acetate. The semi-circular bars can be cut from a piece of card about $\frac{1}{16}$ in. thick, and formed round a pencil.

The small round windows beside the back door, the small round window in the children's bedroom and the semi-circular window above the door in the playroom can all be glazed with Acetate, with no glazing bars.

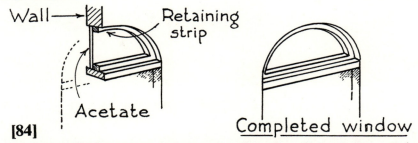

[84]

For the circular and semi-circular windows cut strips of cardboard about $\frac{3}{32}$ in. wide, soak them in water to make them flexible, and then glue the strips to the inner surface of the window apertures, to hold the Acetate in place (see diagram 84).

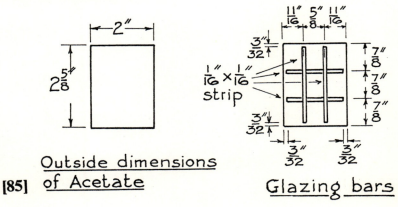

The Garage and Yard Windows: These are made in the same way as the windows in the house. For dimensions see diagram 85.

[85] Outside dimensions of Acetate

Glazing bars

THE CHIMNEY-STACKS AND POTS

Draw a line round each of the stacks exactly $\frac{1}{4}$ in. from the upper surface. Then glue lengths of $\frac{3}{8} \times \frac{1}{8}$ in. stripwood round the stacks so that their upper edges coincide with these lines. After that glue lengths of $\frac{1}{8} \times \frac{1}{8}$ in. strip to the outside (see diagram 86).

Cut three chimney-pots for each stack from $\frac{1}{2}$ in. diameter dowel and glue them on in a central position. A firm bedding for the base of the chimney-pots can be built up with Polyfilla, Alabastine, or plaster of Paris. Finally paint the pots with pale terracotta pink and make a dark circle on the upper surface.

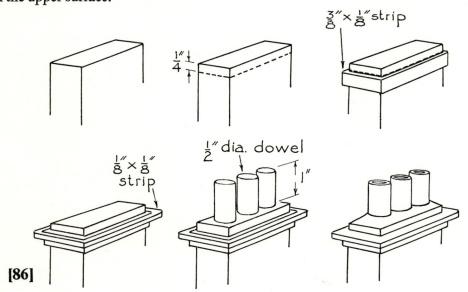

[86]

THE GUTTERS, HOPPERS, DRAINPIPES AND DRAIN COVERS

If fixed carefully, these may be used to locate and secure the front and back walls of the house (see diagrams 87 and 88).

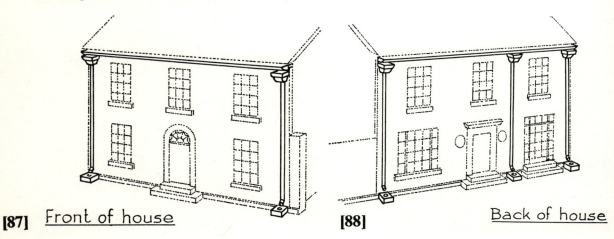

[87] Front of house

[88] Back of house

46

THE GUTTERS, HOPPERS, DRAINPIPES AND DRAIN COVERS

The Gutters: Make these from two lengths of thin picture moulding. If you cannot obtain moulding in a suitable section, you could make the gutters from lengths of quadrant with lengths of stripwood as packing (see diagram 89). Then glue the gutters to the eaves as shown in the diagram.

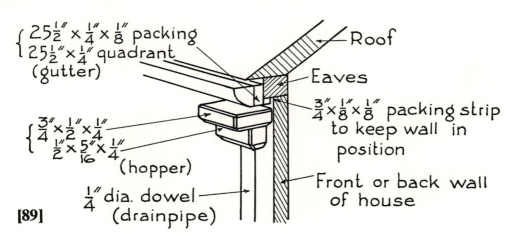

$\{ 25\frac{1}{2}" \times \frac{1}{4}" \times \frac{1}{8}"$ packing
$\{ 25\frac{1}{2}" \times \frac{1}{4}"$ quadrant
(gutter)

$\{ \frac{3}{4}" \times \frac{1}{2}" \times \frac{1}{4}"$
$\{ \frac{1}{2}" \times \frac{5}{16}" \times \frac{1}{4}"$
(hopper)

$\frac{1}{4}"$ dia. dowel
(drainpipe)

[89]

Roof

Eaves

$\frac{3}{4}" \times \frac{1}{8}" \times \frac{1}{8}"$ packing strip to keep wall in position

Front or back wall of house

Hoppers and Drainpipes: For a detailed view of one of the hoppers see diagram 89. No exact length has been given for the downfall drainpipes so that you may shape the lower ends into the conventional kind of outpour spouts.

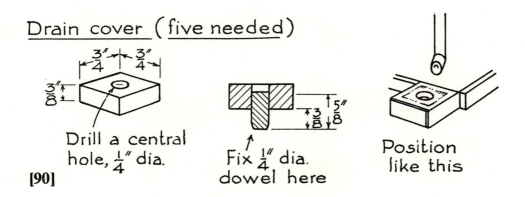

Drain cover (five needed)

$\frac{3}{4}"$ $\frac{3}{4}"$

$\frac{3}{8}"$

Drill a central hole, $\frac{1}{4}"$ dia.

[90]

$\frac{5}{8}"$
$\frac{3}{8}"$

Fix $\frac{1}{4}"$ dia. dowel here

Position like this

Drain Covers: Make these to the dimensions given in diagram 90. If you drill a central $\frac{1}{4}$ in. diameter hole in the bases to receive the projecting pieces of dowel, you can slip the drain covers in and out of position when the front and back walls are being removed.

THE BALUSTRADE

You may either erect a plain, un-
pierced wall round the garden on the
garage roof, or build a balustrade as
shown in diagrams 91–101, which is
generally reminiscent of the balus-
trades on buildings designed by
Robert Adam. How this balustrade
can be made is described below.

First cut the upright blocks (see
diagrams 91, 92 and 93).

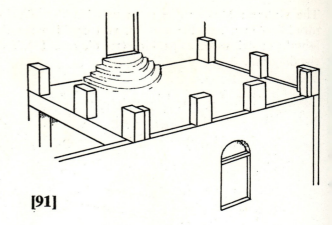

[91]

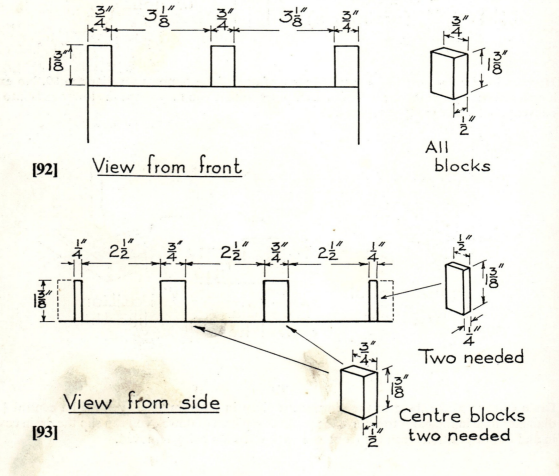

[92] View from front

All blocks

View from side

[93]

Two needed

Centre blocks
two needed

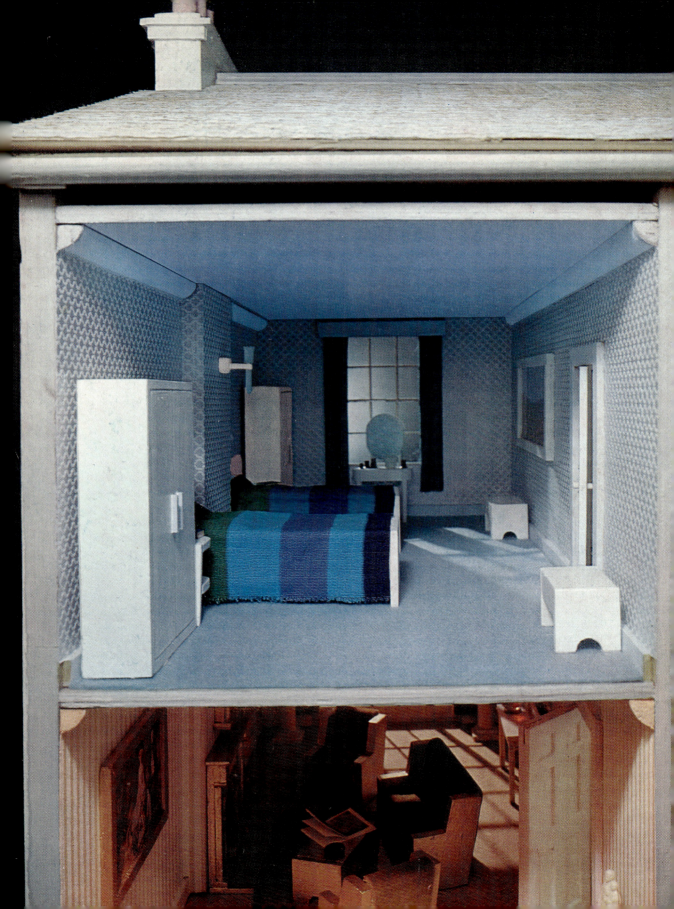

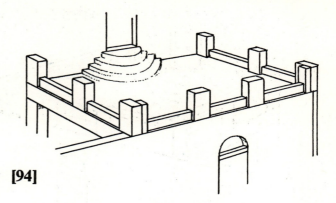

Then make the long base blocks (see diagrams 94, 95 and 96) and drill the ⅛ in. diameter holes in these blocks before you glue them in position.

[94]

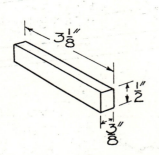

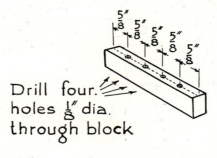

Drill four. holes ⅛" dia. through block

[95]   Four of these blocks are needed

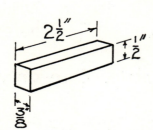

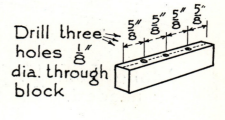

Drill three holes ⅛" dia. through block

[96]   Three of these blocks are needed

The long strips that rest on the upright blocks (see diagrams 97, 98 and 99) should not be glued down until the balusters are fitted (see diagram 100).

THE BALUSTRADE

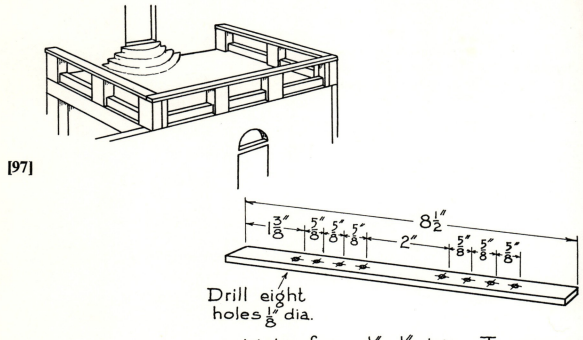

[97]

[98]

Drill eight holes $\frac{1}{8}''$ dia.

Make from $\frac{1}{2}'' \times \frac{1}{8}''$ strip. Two are needed.

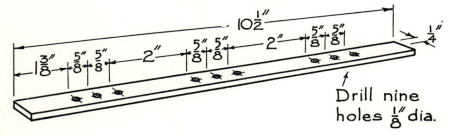

Drill nine holes $\frac{1}{8}''$ dia.

Make from $\frac{1}{2}'' \times \frac{1}{8}''$ strip. One only is needed.

[99]

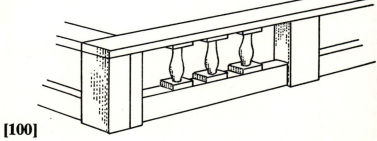

[100]

The balusters shown in the colour plate facing page 48 should be made from $\frac{1}{8}$ in. diameter dowel, two squares of cardboard, and a strip of paper. The drawing on the right of diagram 101 shows how to wind the freely pasted paper round the dowel to produce the required bulge. The holes in the cardboard squares can be made with a leather punch.

If you have access to a woodworkers' lathe, perhaps you could turn the tiny balusters on it, to give the balustrade an even more elegant appearance.

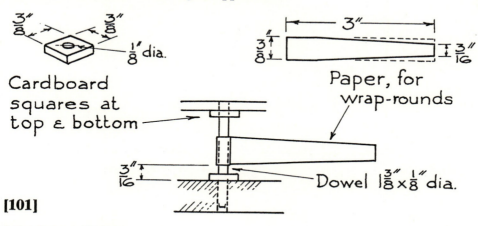

Cardboard squares at top & bottom

Paper, for wrap-rounds

Dowel $1\frac{3}{8}$" × $\frac{1}{8}$" dia.

[101]

A TREE IN A TUB

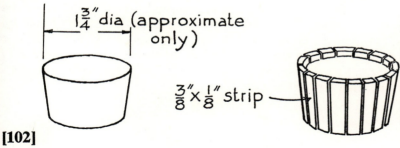

$1\frac{3}{4}$" dia (approximate only)

$\frac{3}{8}$" × $\frac{1}{8}$" strip

[102]

Take a cork approximately $1\frac{3}{4}$ in. in diameter and glue pieces of $\frac{3}{8} \times \frac{1}{8}$ in. stripwood round the sides to represent planking. To represent metal retaining bars, glue paper strips to the outside of the tub (see diagram 102).

Look for a suitable twig and push it into a slit made in the centre of the cork. The blossom can be made from pieces of rock tapioca, attached to the branches with Evostik and then touched with pink water-paint (see diagram 103).

Instead of the tree you can make flowering shrubs from pieces of sponge, foam rubber or loofah.

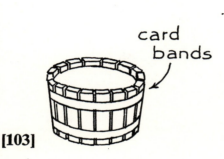

card bands

[103]

THE YARD GATES

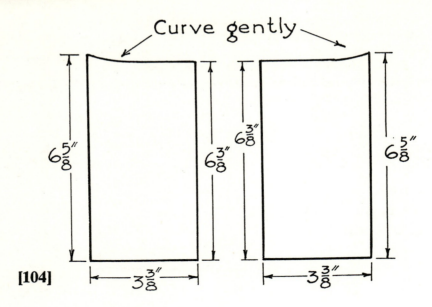

Curve gently

$6\frac{5}{8}''$ $6\frac{3}{8}''$ $6\frac{3}{8}''$ $6\frac{5}{8}''$

[104] $3\frac{3}{8}''$ $3\frac{3}{8}''$

Draw the outside shapes of the gates and of the wrought iron arches above (see diagrams 104 and 105) full size on stiff paper and cut them out to act as guides or templates. Then cut out the Perspex shapes and draw or paint the wrought iron tracery on them in the same way as you did for the banisters on page 31 (see diagrams 106, 107 and 108). Use any design you like—perhaps you have a chance to study examples of work by Jean Tijou in St. Paul's and in several City Churches, or by one of the provincial masters such as Robert Davies of Wrexham whose iron-work is the pride of Leeswood and other country houses.

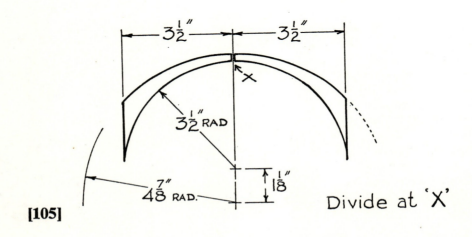

$3\frac{1}{2}''$ $3\frac{1}{2}''$

X

$3\frac{1}{2}''$ RAD

$4\frac{7}{8}''$ RAD. $1\frac{1}{8}''$

[105]   Divide at 'X'

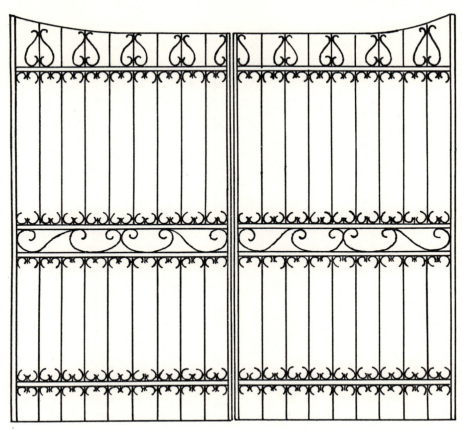

[106]

[107]

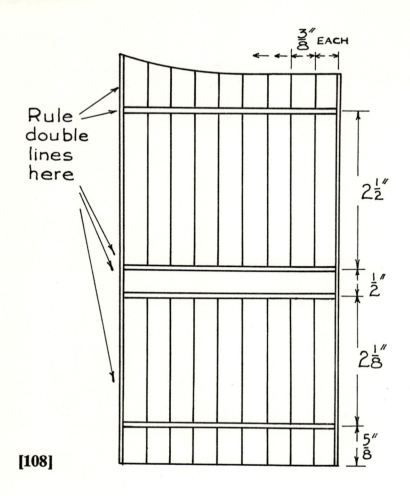

$\frac{3}{8}''$ EACH

Rule
double
lines
here

$2\frac{1}{2}''$

$\frac{1}{2}''$

$2\frac{1}{8}''$

$\frac{5}{8}''$

[108]

Before fixing the gates in position, make two saw cuts down the centre lines of the gate piers for the wide ends of the pieces that make up the arch. When hanging the gates, keep a piece of thick cardboard between the Perspex and the base until the glue is dry, so that the gates will swing freely. The hinges are made of black or blackened tape.

The arch should be fixed in position only after the yard lamp has been made, as the arch pieces may have to be trimmed on the final assembly.

Cut four squares from plywood $\frac{1}{16}$ in. thick (see diagram 110) and four pieces of Perspex or Acetate (see diagram 111). Assemble the pieces as shown in diagram 109 and glue some narrow strips of paper along the edges to look like a metal frame. A cap or cover on the lamp may be made from an upturned button and a small plastic collar-stud.

Assembly of yard lamp

[109]

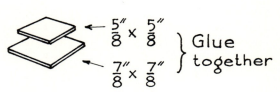

All four squares are made from plywood $\frac{1}{16}''$ thick

← $1'' \times 1''$ ⎫ Glue
← $\frac{3}{4}'' \times \frac{3}{4}''$ ⎬ together

← $\frac{5}{8}'' \times \frac{5}{8}''$ ⎫ Glue
← $\frac{7}{8}'' \times \frac{7}{8}''$ ⎬ together

[110]

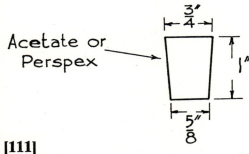

Acetate or Perspex →

$\frac{3}{4}$

$1''$

$\frac{5}{8}''$

[111]

To assemble the arch and the lamp, trim the small ends of the Perspex pieces to the exact lengths and fix the larger ends with Evo-stik in the saw cuts in the gate piers. Make four small brackets from thin cardboard and put the lamp in position (see diagram 112).

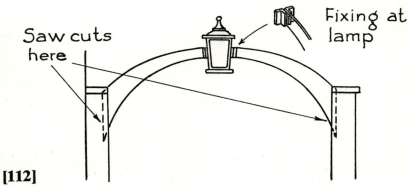

Saw cuts here

Fixing at lamp

[112]

5 Furnishing the Sitting-Room, Hall and Dining-Room

The designs for the furniture in the living-rooms and the hall can be based on those developed by the great eighteenth-century cabinet-makers such as Thomas Chippendale and George Hepplewhite. However, if you are still finding small-scale woodwork difficult to carry out, make the simple furnishings described in this chapter and later you can always replace these with 'collectors' pieces' if you wish.

THE SITTING-ROOM

This is a long-shaped, spacious room with well-proportioned windows and with only a few essential pieces of furniture (see colour plate facing page 32).

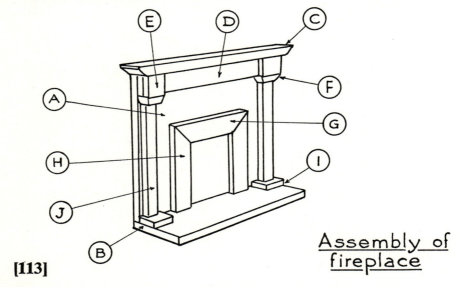

Assembly of fireplace

[113]

The Fireplace: For a simple fireplace (see diagram 113) cut the various pieces from plywood and stripwood to the shapes and dimensions given in diagrams 114 to 117.

Glue Part B to the lower edge of Part A, Part C to the upper edge of Part A, and add Parts D, E, F, G, H and I in their positions shown in diagram 113. Parts J should be glued in position last so that they may be trimmed down if any one of the other parts is slightly oversize.

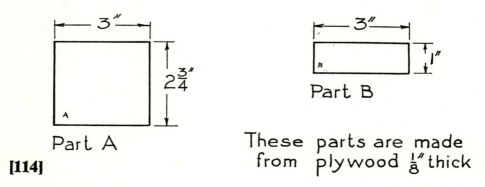

Part A

[114]

Part B

These parts are made from plywood ⅛" thick

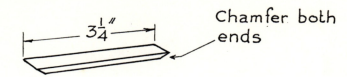

[115] Part C — made from $\frac{1}{2}$″ × $\frac{1}{8}$″ strip

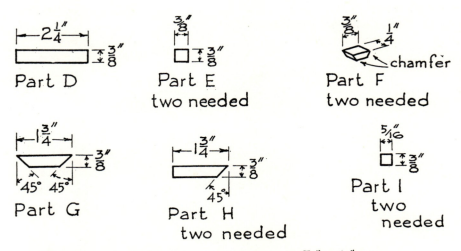

Part D   Part E two needed   Part F two needed

Part G   Part H two needed   Part I two needed

[116] These parts are made from $\frac{3}{8}$″ × $\frac{1}{8}$″ strip

[117] Part J – two needed – make from $\frac{1}{4}$″ × $\frac{1}{8}$″ strip

Add retaining bars, cut from matchsticks or $\frac{1}{16}$ × $\frac{1}{16}$ in. balsa strip, to represent a grate (see colour plate, and diagram 129 on page 61).

Diagram 118 shows a decorated top for the fireplace.

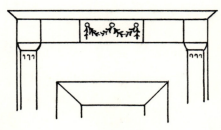

[118]

THE SITTING-ROOM

The Mirror: Above the fireplace you may add a gilded classical mirror. Diagram 119 shows the completed mirror, and diagrams 120 and 121 demonstrate the various steps of the assembly. Finally, the parts should be backed, one by one, to a rectangular piece of plywood (Part K).

Gild the frame with gold paint and fit in some silver paper to represent the glass.

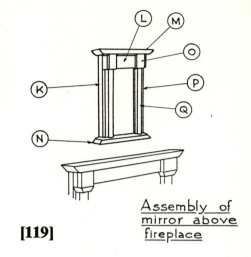

Assembly of mirror above fireplace

[119]

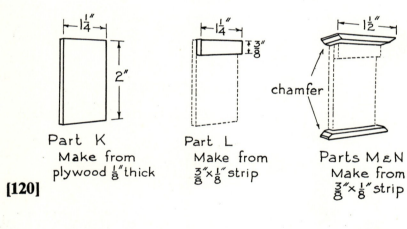

Part K
Make from
plywood $\frac{1}{8}$″ thick

[120]

Part L
Make from
$\frac{3}{8}$″×$\frac{1}{8}$″ strip

chamfer

Parts M & N
Make from
$\frac{3}{8}$″ × $\frac{1}{8}$″ strip

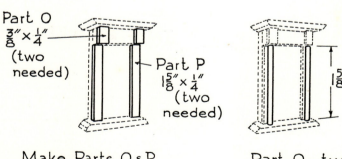

Part O
$\frac{3}{8}$″ × $\frac{1}{4}$″
(two
needed)

Part P
$1\frac{5}{8}$″ × $\frac{1}{4}$″
(two
needed)

Make Parts O & P
from plywood $\frac{1}{16}$″ thick

[121]

Part Q - two
needed - make from
$\frac{1}{8}$″ dia. dowel

58

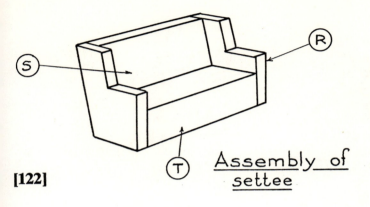

[122]

Assembly of settee

The Settee and Armchairs: For the assembly see diagrams 122 and 125. The dimensions are given in diagrams 123, 124, 126 and 127.

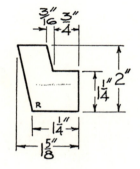

Part R - two needed - make from plywood ¼" thick

[123]

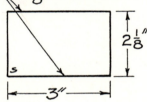

Trim these edges to suit

Part S - one needed- -make from plywood ¼" thick

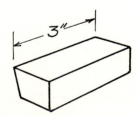

Part T - one needed

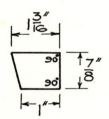

Side view of Part T

[124]

THE SITTING-ROOM

You can draw and cut out the sides of the settee and the sides of the armchairs (Parts R and U) together as they are identical. The back supports (Parts S and V) and the seats (Parts T and W) vary only in their widths and you can plane one long piece of wood to the shape shown in the side views and then subdivide it.

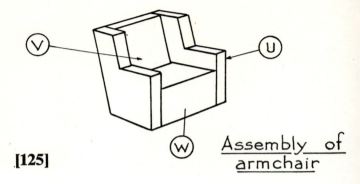

Assembly of armchair

[125]

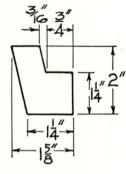

Part U - four needed – make from plywood ¼" thick

[126]

Trim these edges to suit

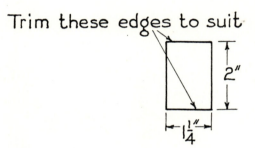

Part V - two needed – – make from plywood ¼" thick

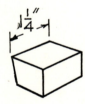

Part W - one needed

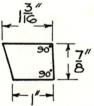

Side view of Part W

[127]

For head-rests glue some lengths of ½ in. diameter half-round dowelling to the tops of the back supports.

Upholster the suite as shown in the colour plate. Paint the side surfaces and glue strips of thick velvet from front to back, following the form of the seats and back supports and suggesting a well-sprung interior. Finally add some tiny cushions.

Fireside
table

Ends-make
from ⅛″ thick
plywood

Body

[128]

A Fireside Table: Size and shape are given in diagram 128. The ends (centre drawing) can be varied and shaped in the form of a lyre.

[129]

Diagram 129 shows the final arrangement of the furniture round the fireplace.

THE SITTING-ROOM

The Pier Tables: An area of wall between two high windows is usually known as a 'pier', and small tables designed to be placed between such windows are known as 'pier tables'.

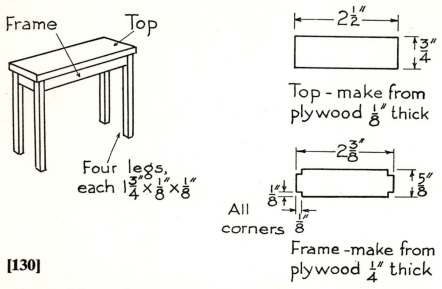

[130]

Two slightly different pier tables, placed against Wall B, are shown in the colour plate. For the dimensions see diagrams 130 and 131.

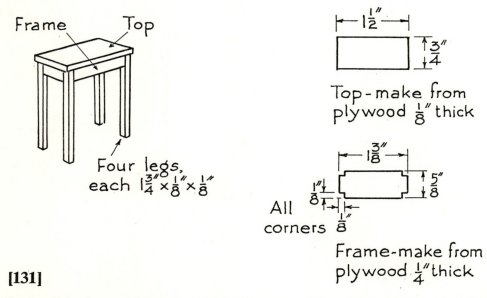

[131]

The body of the lamp on the pier table shown in the background in the colour plate was made by fixing a glass marble to a small brass washer with Evo-stik. The metal top was taken from a bottle of cleansing lotion.

The Sculpture Stands: Make these from ½ in. diameter dowel with square plywood bases and platforms (see diagram 132). To give the stands the appearance of classical columns you may add decorative capitals.

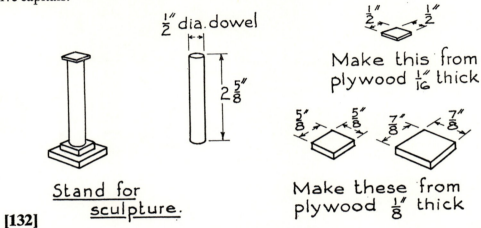

½″ dia. dowel

2⅝″

Stand for sculpture.

[132]

Make this from plywood 1/16″ thick

Make these from plywood ⅛″ thick

Small figures or toy soldiers may represent the sculptures or, if you know a professional sculptor, perhaps you may get two original miniature art works. Or you could take miniature dolls and adapt these with Polyfilla or plaster of Paris to make them look like genuine works of art.

Pictures on the Wall: You can choose these from papers, magazines, art gallery catalogues, etc. Allow a suitable margin for attaching the frame when cutting out the pictures, and back each with a rectangular piece of plywood (see diagram 133).

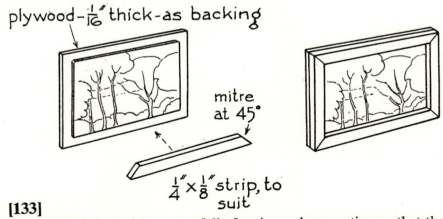

plywood—1/16″ thick—as backing

mitre at 45°

¼″ × ⅛″ strip, to suit

[133]

It is important to choose pictures carefully for size and proportion so that they will hang in a pleasing way with the structural features and furnishing of the room. Diagram 129 shows how pictures can be arranged on each side of the fireplace to achieve a satisfactory composition.

If there are pictures of different sizes and proportions in the same room, their arrangement can be simplified by making sure that the lower edges of the frames are at identical distances from the floor.

THE HALL

[134]

Diagram 134 shows how a picture, that is wider than high, can be hung satisfactorily near the longer pier table.

THE HALL

Shape and dimensions for a small semi-circular table in the hall are given in diagram 135.

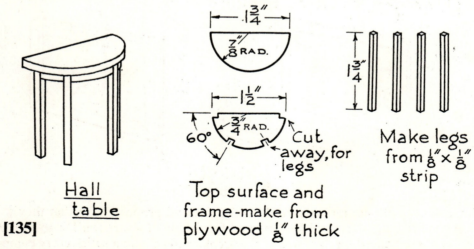

Hall table

[135]

In the colour plate facing page 17 a fan-shaped floral arrangement can be seen on the table, made from small pieces of dried grass and scraps of foam rubber, which helps to furnish the hall without taking up much space.

The Fireplace: This can be made in exactly the same way as the fireplace in the sitting-room.

The Dining-Room Table: The table shown in diagram 136 is a simplified version of an eighteenth-century design. For the shapes and dimensions of the various parts that make it up see diagram 137. The hinged leaves at the table sides allow an extension of the top surface.

Assembly of dining table

[136]

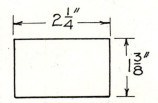

Top surface—
make from plywood
$\frac{1}{8}$" thick

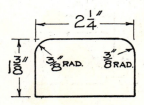

Drop leaf—two
needed—make from
plywood $\frac{1}{8}$" thick

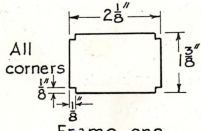

All corners

Frame—one
needed—make from
plywood $\frac{1}{4}$" thick

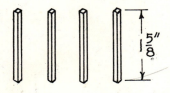

Legs—make
from $\frac{1}{8}$"×$\frac{1}{8}$" strip

[137]

THE DINING-ROOM

The Chairs: A finished chair is shown in diagram 138, and shapes and dimensions of the various parts are given in diagrams 139 and 140. You can make six such chairs, two perhaps with arm-rests, and leave one in the back hall.

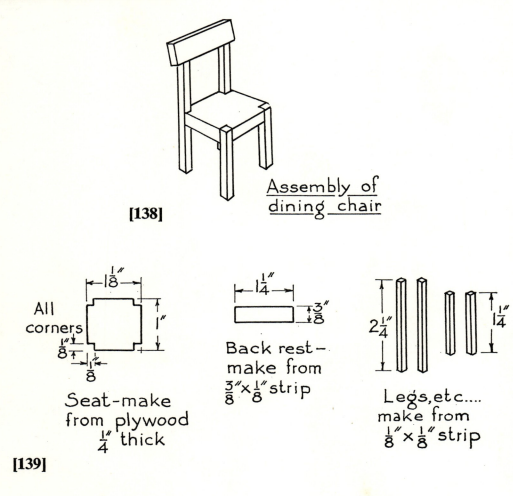

Assembly of dining chair

[138]

Seat—make from plywood $\frac{1}{4}$" thick

All corners $\frac{1}{8}$"

Back rest— make from $\frac{3}{8}$"×$\frac{1}{8}$" strip

Legs, etc.... make from $\frac{1}{8}$"×$\frac{1}{8}$" strip

[139]

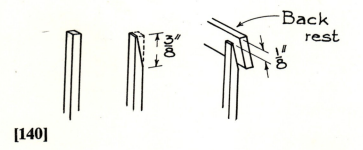

Back rest

[140]

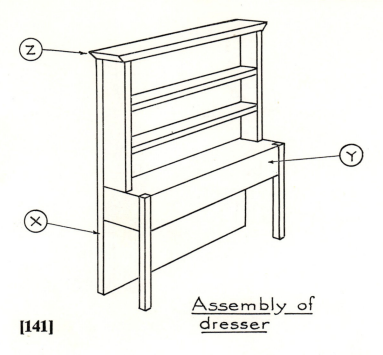

Z

Y

X

Assembly of
dresser

[141]

The Dresser: For shape and dimensions see diagrams 141, 142, and 143. On the front of Part Y mark the outlines of drawers and add bent wire handles.

The 'gold plates', which can be seen on the shelves in the colour plate facing page 33, were made from brass washers backed with furnishing fabric.

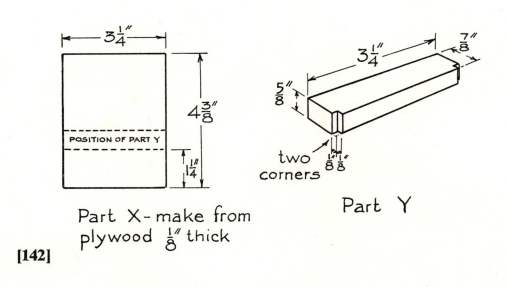

$3\frac{1}{4}''$

$4\frac{3}{8}''$

POSITION OF PART Y

$1\frac{1}{4}''$

Part X - make from
plywood $\frac{1}{8}''$ thick

$3\frac{1}{4}''$

$\frac{7}{8}''$

$\frac{5}{8}''$

two $1\frac{1}{8}''\frac{1}{8}''$
corners

Part Y

[142]

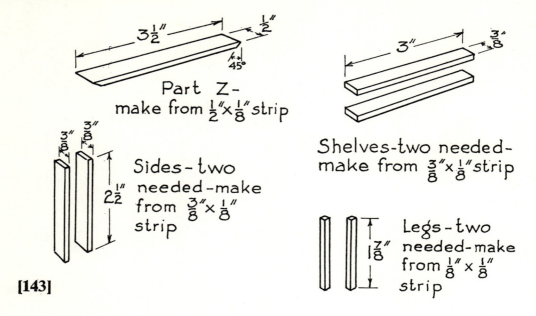

Part Z—
make from ½"×⅛" strip

Sides-two
needed-make
from ⅜"×⅛"
strip

[143]

Shelves-two needed-
make from ⅜"×⅛" strip

Legs-two
needed-make
from ⅛"×⅛"
strip

The Serving Hatch: This has been cut into Wall F between kitchen and dining-room. Below the hatch glue a piece of ⅜ × ⅜ in. quadrant and a piece of ½ × ⅛ in. stripwood to make a serving shelf (see diagram 144).

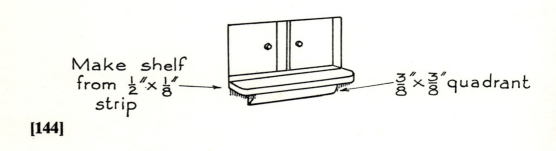

Make shelf
from ½"×⅛"
strip

⅜"×⅜" quadrant

[144]

6 Furnishing the Kitchen

There are two important utility units in the kitchen—the sink unit with a pull-out surface and an eye-level cupboard above, which stands against Wall D, and a storage unit which stands against Wall C. Make these two units first so that you can carry on with the smaller furnishings while the adhesives are drying.

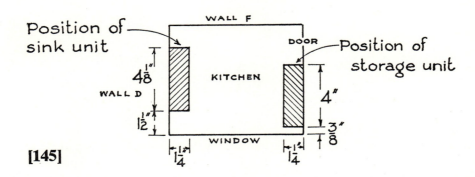

[145]

Diagram 145 shows the suggested positions of the units on the floor.

The Sink Unit: The assembled unit can be seen on diagram 146.

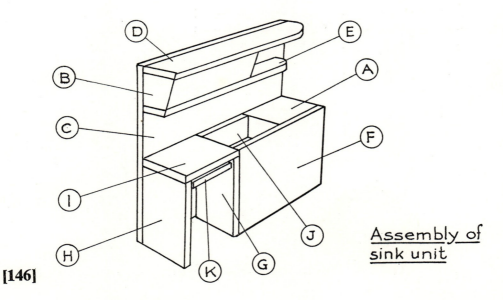

Assembly of sink unit

[146]

THE KITCHEN

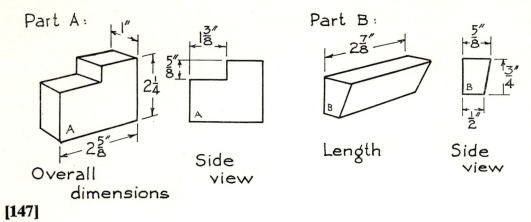

Part A:

Overall dimensions

Side view

Part B:

Length

Side view

[147]

Cut two parts from small blocks of wood to the dimensions given in diagram 147, and nine parts from ⅛ in. thick plywood as shown in diagram 148.

Assemble Parts D and E to Part B first, and then Part A to Part C. The other parts can be positioned later. The pull-out working surface, Part K, can be made to run on two lengths of matchstick glued to Parts G and H.

Before painting the kitchen furniture, mark the outlines of sliding glass-doors on Part B of the sink unit, and of some under-sink cupboard doors on Part F. Glue or cement small pieces of matchstick or balsa strip to the cupboard doors to represent handles.

Apply to the working surfaces pieces of Fablon or similar material, or small pieces of thin Vinyl flooring tile, and coat the sink and the draining-board with silver paper to represent stainless steel.

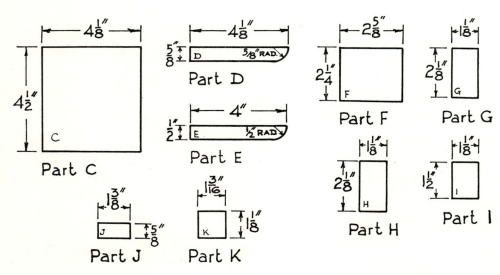

Part C

Part D

Part E

Part F

Part G

Part H

Part I

Part J

Part K

[148] These parts are made from plywood ⅛″ thick

You can add to the sink unit a towel hanger made from a pronged metal hair clip, and the plastic top from a cardboard wine-gum holder may represent a rinsing bowl. The taps in the sink unit shown in the colour plate facing page 48, for example, were made from two small pieces cut from a broken plastic toy.

The Storage Unit: Cut the various parts to the shapes and dimensions given in diagrams 150 and 151, and assemble as shown in diagram 149.

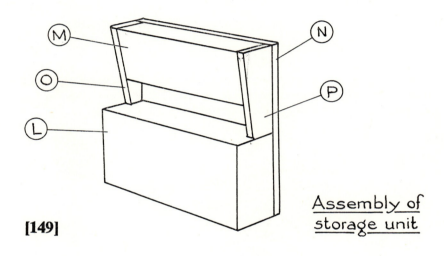

[149]

Assembly of
storage unit

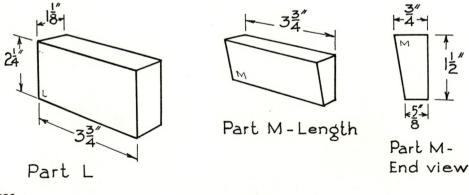

Part L

Part M - Length

Part M -
End view

[150]

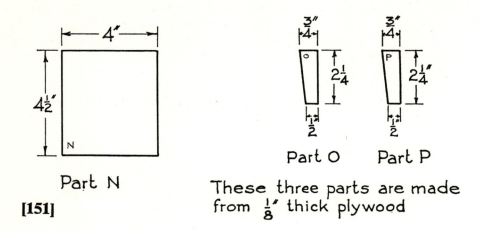

Part N

Part O   Part P

These three parts are made from $\frac{1}{8}''$ thick plywood

[151]

Before you paint the unit, mark the outlines of sliding glass-doors on the upper part, and of two or three separate compartments on the lower part. Add some handles made from matchsticks or square sections of balsa strip (see diagram 152).

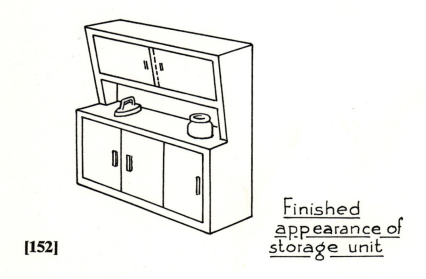

[152]

Finished appearance of storage unit

Among your metal or plastic oddments you may find something suitable to make dishes, bowls or any other small items of kitchen equipment to put on the working surface of the unit. The flat-iron which is just visible on the colour plate, was taken from a discarded game of Monopoly.

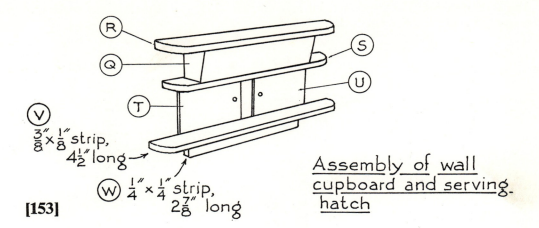

Ⓥ $\frac{3}{8}$" x $\frac{1}{8}$" strip, 4$\frac{1}{2}$" long →

Ⓦ $\frac{1}{4}$" x $\frac{1}{4}$" strip, 2$\frac{7}{8}$" long

Assembly of wall cupboard and serving hatch

[153]

The Wall Cupboard and the Serving Hatch: Above the serving hatch in the wall between the dining-room and the kitchen you could place a small cupboard (see diagrams 153 and 154).

When assembling the serving hatch in the kitchen, set Parts S and V about $\frac{1}{16}$ in. forward, away from the wall, so that the hatch doors, Parts T and U, can slide, and rub with some fine glass-paper along the edges of the doors to ensure that they go smoothly.

Drill a hole in each hatch door and insert small pieces of matchstick to represent handles.

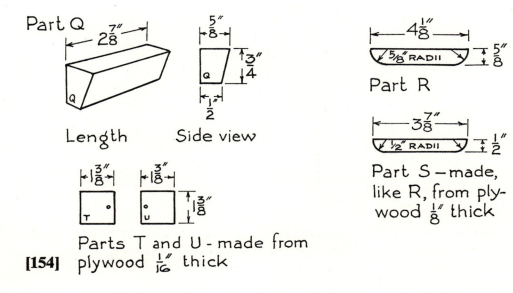

Part Q

Length   Side view

Parts T and U – made from

[154] plywood $\frac{1}{16}$" thick

Part R

Part S – made, like R, from plywood $\frac{1}{8}$" thick

73

THE KITCHEN

The Kitchen Table: For the dimensions see diagram 155. The surface of the table may be covered with a piece of thin Vinyl floor tile.

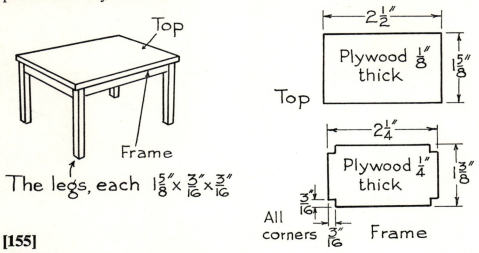

Top

Frame

The legs, each $1\frac{5}{8}'' \times \frac{3}{16}'' \times \frac{3}{16}''$

Top

$2\frac{1}{2}''$

Plywood $\frac{1}{8}''$ thick

$1\frac{5}{8}''$

$2\frac{1}{4}''$

Plywood $\frac{1}{4}''$ thick

$1\frac{3}{8}''$

All corners $\frac{3}{16}$

$\frac{3}{16}$

Frame

[155]

The Kitchen Stools: The black-seated stools seen in the colour plate were made from plastic screw-on caps of Indian ink bottles. The hollows on the underside of the caps were filled with Polyfilla, and lengths of $\frac{1}{8} \times \frac{1}{8}$ in. stripwood were pressed into this to act as legs.

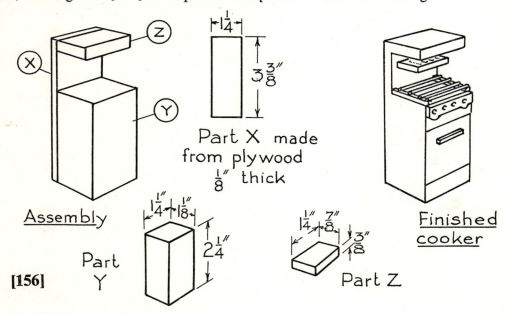

Assembly

Part X made from plywood $\frac{1}{8}''$ thick

$\frac{1}{4}''$

$3\frac{3}{8}''$

Part Y

$\frac{1}{4}''$ $\frac{1}{8}''$

$2\frac{1}{4}''$

Part Z

$\frac{1}{4}''$ $\frac{7}{8}''$

$\frac{3}{8}''$

Finished cooker

[156]

The Cooker: For the shape and dimensions see diagram 156. The eye-level grill can be made from pieces of plastic, and the bars for kettles and saucepans from balsa wood strip. A long black strip of plastic may represent the row of dials by which the heat is controlled.

The Washer: Cut a block of wood to the dimensions given in diagram 157, paint the cover and the makers' badge in some bright colour and add a tap in the lower half of the washer. You may put the washing machine in the recess under the working surface in the sink.

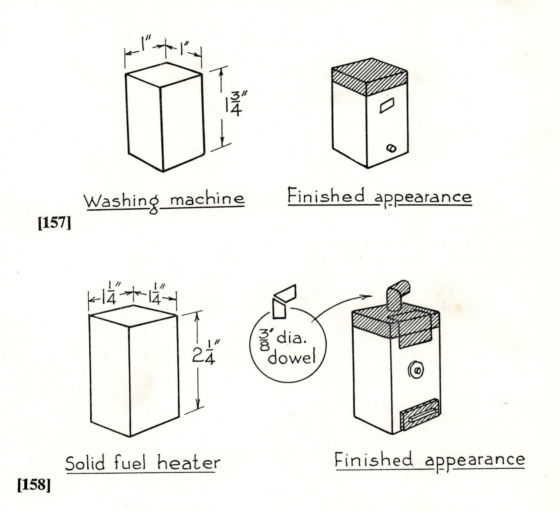

Washing machine   Finished appearance

[157]

Solid fuel heater   Finished appearance

[158]

The Solid Fuel Heater: Work to the dimensions given in diagram 158, add a few lines, two pieces of dowel, and some small details cut from wood strip, as seen on the drawing on the right of the diagram. The portions shaded with slanting lines should be painted black (you could use 'blackboard black' which is sold at most ironmongers' and decorators' material shops), the rest should be white. The heater can be placed between the sink unit and the back wall of the kitchen.

7 Furnishing the Parents' Bedroom

The largest room upstairs is the parents' bedroom. It extends from the front wall of the house to the back wall and has two big windows.

The furnishings described in this chapter are kept very simple, so that they can be easily adapted. For example, instead of the twin beds you could make a large four-poster bed, or you could plan the room round a pair of Victorian brass-knobbed bedsteads.

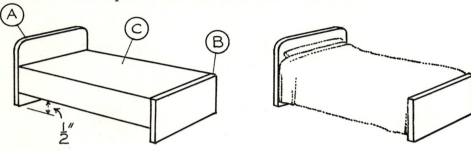

[159] Assembly of parent's bed   Finished appearance

The Twin Beds: The assembly and a completed bed are shown in diagram 159. Cut the parts to the dimensions given in diagram 160, and finish the headboards by rounding off the top corners. Before applying adhesive, mark on Parts A and B the correct position of Part C. Pillows and some bedclothes will complete the twin beds.

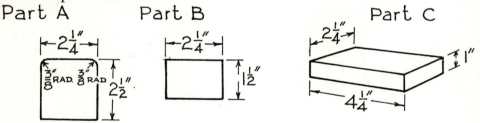

Part A   Part B   Part C

Make Parts A and B from
[160] plywood $\frac{1}{8}''$ thick

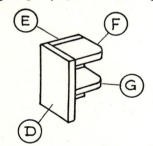

Parts D & E   Parts F & G

Assembly of   All four parts are made
[161] bedside shelves   from plywood $\frac{1}{8}''$ thick

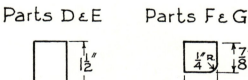

The Bedside Shelves: Cut the plywood parts and assemble as shown in diagram 161.

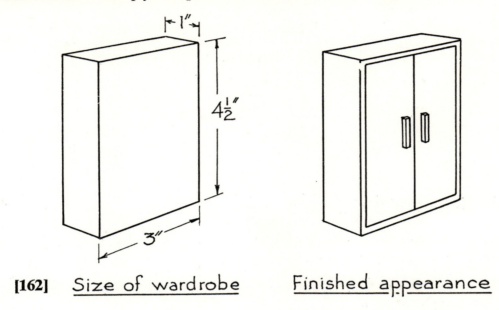

[162]   Size of wardrobe   Finished appearance

The Wardrobes: Cut two blocks of wood to the dimensions given in diagram 162 and before painting these pieces of furniture, draw the outlines of the doors on each wardrobe and add two handles.

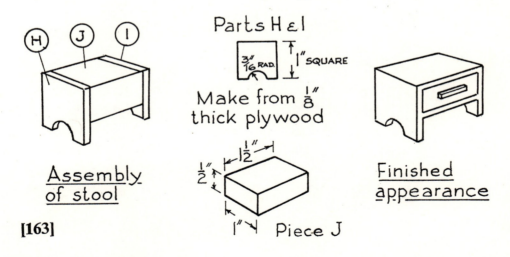

Parts H & I

Make from $\frac{1}{8}$" thick plywood

Assembly of stool

[163]

Piece J

Finished appearance

The Stools: For shape and dimensions see diagram 163. You may vary the shape of the ends, Part H and I, and suggest a drawer by marking its outlines on one side of the stool, and by adding a stripwood handle.

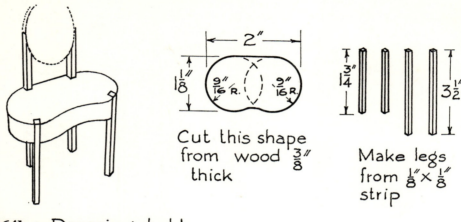

Cut this shape from wood $\frac{3}{8}$" thick

Make legs from $\frac{1}{8}$" × $\frac{1}{8}$" strip

[164]   Dressing table

The Dressing-Table: The dimensions for a kidney-shaped dressing-table are given in diagram 164. You may conceal the legs by fastening a small piece of finely patterned drapery round the lower part of the table.

Cut the mirror from $\frac{1}{16}$ in. thick plywood to any desired size and shape, and use silver paper to represent the mirror glass.

On the dressing-table shown in the colour plate facing page 49 some small purple expanding-rivets represent cosmetic containers, pots and bottles, and a white screw-on top of an ointment tube is used to represent a face-powder pot.

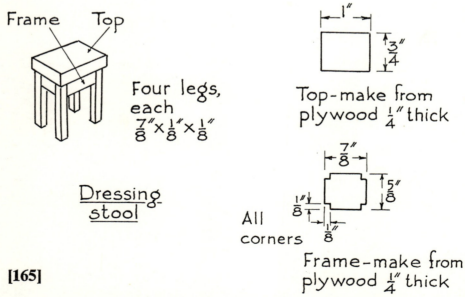

Frame   Top

Four legs, each $\frac{7}{8}$" × $\frac{1}{8}$" × $\frac{1}{8}$"

Top—make from plywood $\frac{1}{4}$" thick

Dressing stool

All corners

Frame—make from plywood $\frac{1}{4}$" thick

[165]

Shape and dimensions for a stool in front of the dressing-table are shown in diagram 165.

8 Furnishing the Children's Bedroom and Playroom

THE BEDROOM

The beds dealt with in this chapter are twin beds. You may, however, provide extra floor space by making bunk beds, one bed on top of the other.

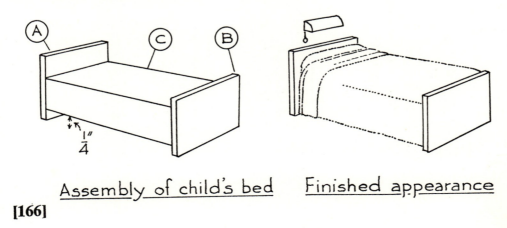

Assembly of child's bed   Finished appearance

[166]

The Beds: The assembly and one of the finished beds are shown in diagram 166 (see also colour plate facing page 64). For the shape and dimensions of the various parts see diagram 167. You can curve the corners of the headboards or decorate them with cut-out animal motifs.

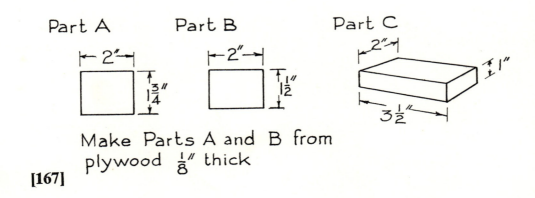

Part A   Part B   Part C

Make Parts A and B from plywood $\frac{1}{8}''$ thick

[167]

Above the beds you can add bed-head lightshades, cut from $\frac{3}{8} \times \frac{3}{8}$ in. quadrant and at the final assembly glued to the wall.

THE CHILDREN'S BEDROOM

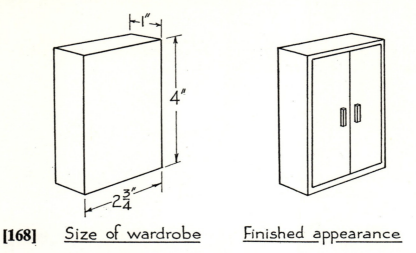

[168] <u>Size of wardrobe</u>   <u>Finished appearance</u>

The Wardrobe: Cut this from one fairly large piece of wood to the shape and dimensions given in diagram 168. Before you paint the wardrobe, mark the outlines of the doors and add two handles.

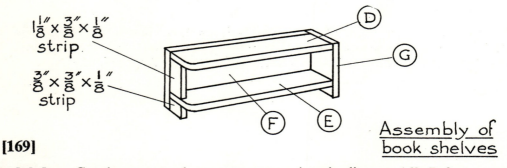

$1\frac{1}{8}'' \times \frac{3}{8}'' \times \frac{1}{8}''$ strip

$\frac{3}{8}'' \times \frac{3}{8}'' \times \frac{1}{8}''$ strip

[169]   <u>Assembly of</u> <u>book shelves</u>

The Bookshelves: Cut the parts to the measurements given in diagram 169. Before assembling the shelves, round off the corners of Parts D and E (see diagram 170) to match the round window above.

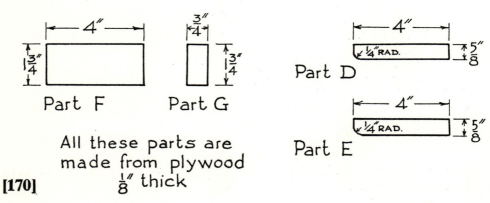

Part F   Part G   Part D

All these parts are made from plywood $\frac{1}{8}''$ thick

Part E

[170]

80

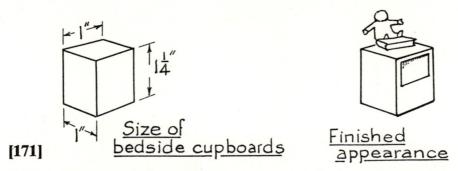

[171] Size of bedside cupboards

Finished appearance

The Bedside Cupboards and the Window-Seat: These are cut from small blocks of wood to the dimensions given in diagrams 171 and 172. To finish the bedside cupboards, mark the outlines of a drawer and add a felt or velvet top to the window-seat.

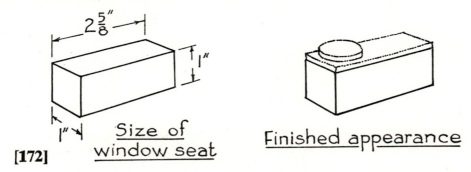

[172] Size of window seat

Finished appearance

If you like, you can look in magazines or illustrated papers for a suitable motif to make an eye-catching mural decoration. Cut this out and paste it to the wall as shown in diagram 173.

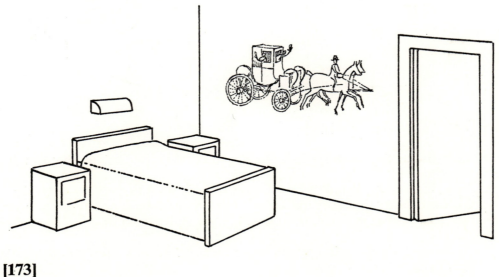

[173]

THE PLAYROOM

This lies next to the children's bedroom and has direct access to the roof-garden over the garage.

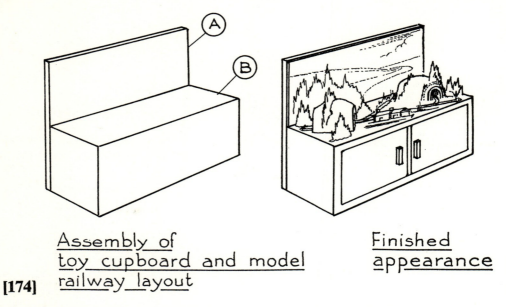

Assembly of
toy cupboard and model
[174] railway layout

Finished
appearance

The Toy Cupboard: As shown in the colour plate facing page 48, a large display board can be fitted at the back of this cupboard, with a landscape background, so that the top surface can be used for a realistic model railway layout (see diagrams 174 and 175).

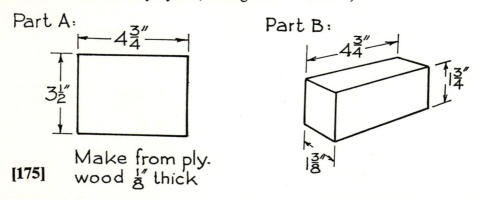

Part A:

$4\frac{3}{4}''$

$3\frac{1}{2}''$

Make from ply.
[175] wood $\frac{1}{8}''$ thick

Part B:

$4\frac{3}{4}''$

$1\frac{3}{4}''$

$1\frac{3}{8}''$

Instead of painting the landscape background, you could take a colour photograph from a book or a magazine.

The hills and glades of the railway layout can be built up with Polyfilla or papier mâché. Cut up small cardboard tubes for tunnels, and make some hedges and trees from scraps of green sponge, foam rubber or wool. Buildings, bridges and the railway wagons may be cut from balsa wood strip.

Instead of a model railway layout you could build a small-scale replica of the miniature house and put this on the toy cupboard.

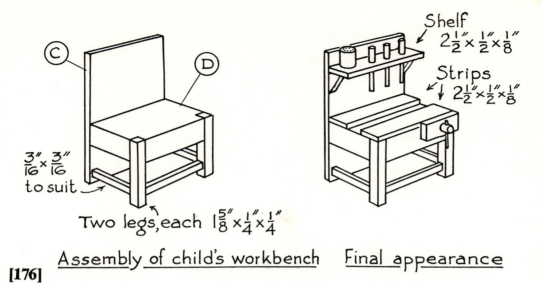

Shelf $2\frac{1}{2}" \times \frac{1}{2}" \times \frac{1}{8}"$

Strips $2\frac{1}{2}" \times \frac{1}{2}" \times \frac{1}{8}"$

$\frac{3}{16}" \times \frac{3}{16}"$ to suit

Two legs, each $1\frac{5}{8}" \times \frac{1}{4}" \times \frac{1}{4}"$

Assembly of child's workbench   Final appearance

[176]

The Workbench: Diagrams 176 and 177 show the dimensions of the various parts and the final appearance of this piece of furniture. You can add small tools—chisels and gouges, a saw made from a piece of hack-saw blade with a plywood or balsa wood handle, or a vice, made from $\frac{3}{8} \times \frac{1}{8}$ in. strip and $\frac{1}{8}$ in. diameter dowel. Drill some holes in the shelf at the back of the workbench and place there some of these tools.

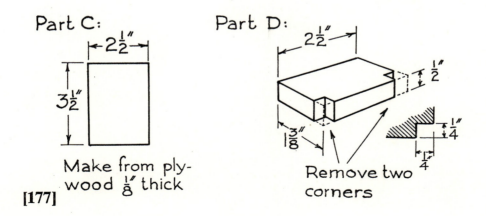

Part C:

$2\frac{1}{2}"$

$3\frac{1}{2}"$

Make from plywood $\frac{1}{8}"$ thick

Part D:

$2\frac{1}{2}"$

$\frac{1}{2}"$

$1\frac{3}{8}"$

$\frac{1}{4}"$

$\frac{1}{4}"$

Remove two corners

[177]

83

THE PLAYROOM

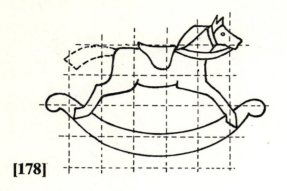

[178]

The Rocking-Horse: Cut two pieces of plywood $\frac{1}{16}$ in. thick to the shape shown in diagram 178. The dotted lines represent half inch squares that will help you to reproduce the outlines of the horse on the plywood pieces. Between the two pieces glue a wooden block cut to the size given in diagram 179. Taper the block slightly to splay the rockers (end view). This will increase the stability of the rocking-horse.

[179]   About $\frac{1}{2}"$ End view

Finish the rocking-horse by working Polyfilla, plaster of Paris or some other hard-setting material into the interstices between the block and the plywood pieces. Add a mane and a tail, made from knitting wool or teased-out strings, and finally paint the horse.

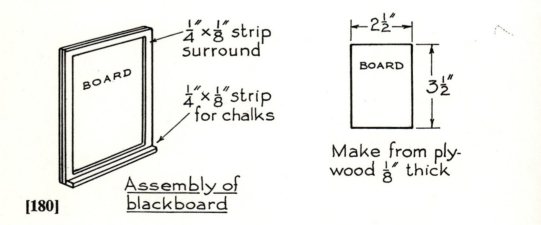

[180]   Assembly of blackboard

$\frac{1}{4}" \times \frac{1}{8}"$ strip surround

$\frac{1}{4}" \times \frac{1}{8}"$ strip for chalks

Make from plywood $\frac{1}{8}"$ thick

The Blackboard: For dimensions and assembly see diagram 180. Paint the drawing surface black, and add some white-painted pieces of matchstick on the protruding ledge to represent chalk, as well as a little duster hanging beside the blackboard.

84

9 Furnishing the Bathroom, Back Hall and Cloakroom

The bathroom upstairs and the cloakroom on the ground floor are furnished in almost exactly the same way, but you may add a little variety to the toilet arrangements by designing a different suite for one of the two rooms. You can incorporate some Victorian flower-covered chinaware or, if you prefer, some modern china with contemporary designs as shown at the Building Centre, Store Street, W.C.1.

THE BATHROOM

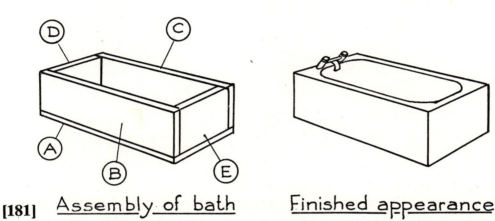

[181] Assembly of bath   Finished appearance

The Bath: For assembly and finished appearance see diagram 181. Cut the five pieces (see diagram 182) from ¼ in. thick plywood and give the inside surface a series of smooth curves with Polyfilla or plaster of Paris.

Short lengths of ⅛ in. diameter dowel or pieces of wire may represent the taps, and from two strips of balsa wood and a rectangular piece of Acetate a movable tray for sponges and soap can be made.

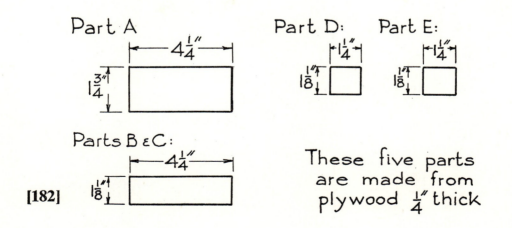

Part A

Part D: Part E:

Parts B &C:

[182]

These five parts are made from plywood ¼″ thick

85

THE BATHROOM

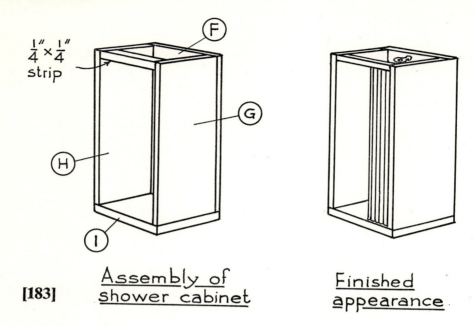

$\frac{1''}{4} \times \frac{1''}{4}$ strip

[183] Assembly of shower cabinet

Finished appearance

The Shower Cabinet: The dimensions for the walls and the floor of the shower cabinet next to the bath (see diagram 183) are given in diagram 184. A $\frac{1}{2}$ in. diameter washer, fixed to a piece of stripwood, can represent the circular water spray, and the curtain can be made from a piece of a plastic spongebag or by gluing some drinking-straws together.

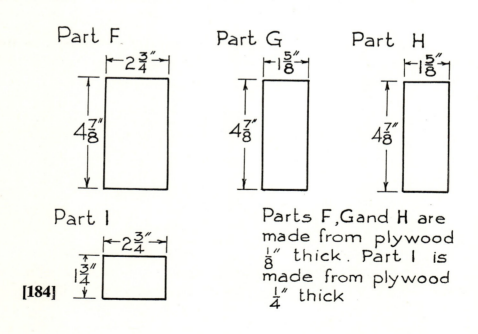

Part F — $2\frac{3}{4}''$ — $4\frac{7}{8}''$

Part G — $1\frac{5}{8}''$ — $4\frac{7}{8}''$

Part H — $1\frac{5}{8}''$ — $4\frac{7}{8}''$

Part I — $2\frac{3}{4}''$ — $1\frac{3}{4}''$

[184]

Parts F, G and H are made from plywood $\frac{1}{8}''$ thick. Part I is made from plywood $\frac{1}{4}''$ thick

The Wash-Basin: The assembled and finished basin can be seen in diagram 185. Part J, the bowl, is shown in two stages in diagram 186.

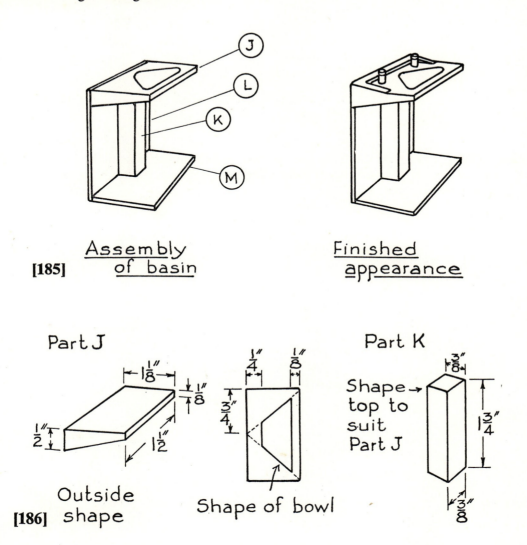

[185] Assembly of basin — Finished appearance

Part J

[186] Outside shape — Shape of bowl — Part K — Shape top to suit Part J

First, cut the wood to the shape shown on the left, and then hollow out the bowl as shown on the right. Then glue a rectangle of plywood $\frac{1}{16}$ in. thick to the underside and fill up and round off the corners with Polyfilla or plaster of Paris. Taps may be added as before to the bath.

Round the back of the basin glue some small pieces of $\frac{1}{8} \times \frac{1}{16}$ in. stripwood to represent the raised mouldings that prevent surplus water from flowing away.

The two rectangles of plywood (diagram 187) behind and below the central column of the wash-basin are meant for purposes of support only, and if the wash-basin is fixed permanently to the floor, you will not need them.

87

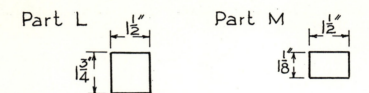

Part L   Part M

Both these parts are made from
plywood $\frac{1}{16}$" thick

[187]

Sanitary Fittings: Diagram 188 shows the assembled and finished sanitary fittings; shape and dimensions of the various parts are given in diagrams 189 and 190. Tape hinges can be used to fasten Parts S and T to Part P.

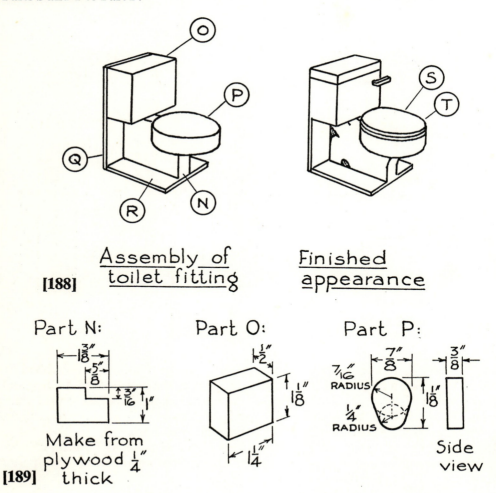

Assembly of   Finished
toilet fitting   appearance

[188]

Part N: Part O: Part P:

Make from
plywood $\frac{1}{4}$"   Side
thick   view

[189]

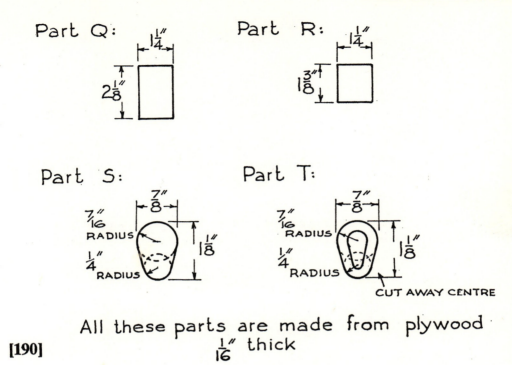

Part Q: Part R:

Part S: Part T:

CUT AWAY CENTRE

All these parts are made from plywood
$\frac{1}{16}$" thick

[190]

By choosing different colours or patterns you may add a little variety to the interiors of the cloakroom decorations and the bathroom on the first floor.

Towel Rails: For the dimensions and the assembled rails see diagrams 191 and 192. Drill the sides of both fittings to take $\frac{1}{16}$ in. diameter dowel.

Glue the smaller rail to the side of the shower next to the bath, and the long single rail to the wall between the shower and the door.

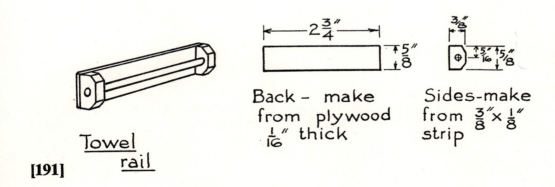

Towel
rail

Back – make
from plywood
$\frac{1}{16}$" thick

Sides–make
from $\frac{3}{8}$" x $\frac{1}{8}$"
strip

[191]

THE BATHROOM

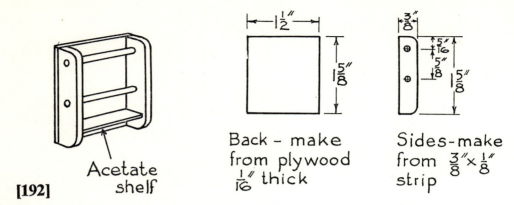

[192]

Acetate shelf

Back – make from plywood $\frac{1}{16}$" thick

Sides – make from $\frac{3}{8}$" × $\frac{1}{8}$" strip

A Stool: Make the stool to the dimensions given in diagram 193, and later, when you are soft-furnishing, put a rectangular piece of felt or other thick material on the floor near the stool to represent a bath mat.

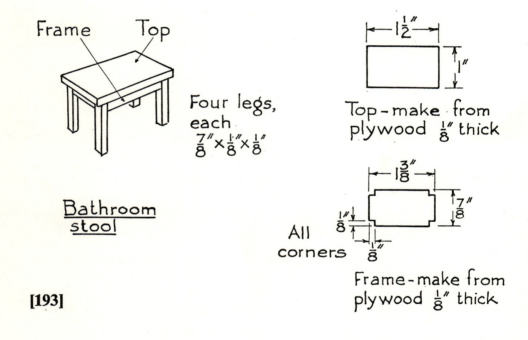

Frame   Top

Four legs, each $\frac{7}{8}$" × $\frac{1}{8}$" × $\frac{1}{8}$"

Top – make from plywood $\frac{1}{8}$" thick

All corners $\frac{1}{8}$"

Frame – make from plywood $\frac{1}{8}$" thick

Bathroom stool

[193]

The Screen: The sanitary fittings in the bathroom may be screened off so that the room appears to be divided into two separate zones. Make a frame from $\frac{1}{4}$ × $\frac{1}{8}$ in. strip and use for the screen a piece of Acetate or Perspex, $5\frac{1}{8}$ × 2 in. wide (see diagram 194).

If, later, you want to be able to slide the bathroom out of the house, you must glue the screen to the floor instead of to the wall.

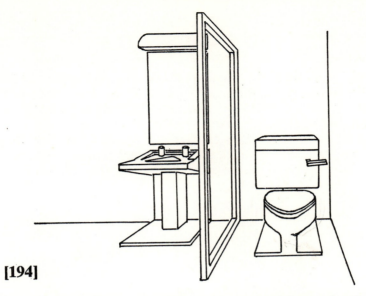

[194]

A Mirror: Above the wash-basin you can fit a flat silver paper mirror, and a shaving-light made from $\frac{3}{8} \times \frac{3}{8}$ in. quadrant (see diagram 194). Other details such as a tooth-brush holder can be added to complete the furnishings of the bathroom.

THE BACK HALL AND THE CLOAKROOM

As the wash-basin and sanitary fittings in the cloakroom downstairs are almost the same as those in the bathroom, only a few additions to the furnishings are suggested.

A Toilet Cupboard: The cupboard in the room shown in the colour plate facing page 65 is made from a cream-coloured plastic razor-blade holder. If you cannot find anything suitable ready made, cut a small piece of wood to your own design, add a silver paper mirror to the front surface and glue the completed cupboard above the hand basin in the cloakroom.

A Stick Stand: This can be made from a ladies' translucent haircurler, cut down to a suitable size and fitted with a circular base. The stick stand in the colour plate was fitted to a base made from the plastic end of a tooth-brush carton. Walking-sticks can be made from hairpins or short lengths of dowel.

Pegs: Drill a row of holes in a strip of wood, fit some small pieces of $\frac{1}{16}$ in. diameter dowel in the holes, and glue the pegs to the wall in the back hall.

10 Finishing the Woodwork, Painting and Decorating, Soft Furnishing, Floor Coverings, and Lighting

FILLING

A quick survey of the fabric of the miniature house and of the pieces of furniture will reveal a number of small holes, cracks, gaps, depressions, and other surface flaws. Before you start painting and decorating, fill these holes and gaps with one of the positive-bond preparations sold at most household stores and decorators' material shops.

Mix the powder with water following the directions on the packet, and feed the paste into the holes with some suitable implement such as the end of a penknife. A useful feeder can be made by shaving down the end of an old paint-brush handle (see diagram 195).

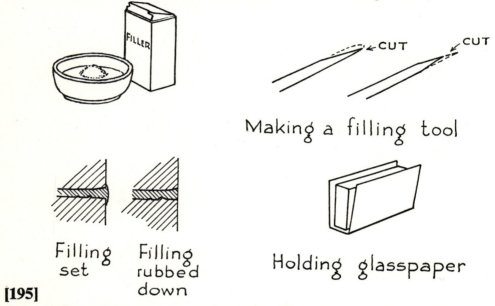

Making a filling tool

Filling set   Filling rubbed down   Holding glasspaper

[195]

Most proprietary fillers are supposed not to shrink as they dry or set, but it is better to leave the made-up surface slightly higher than actually required and to rub back the surplus material with a fine-grade glass-paper after all the moisture has evaporated (see diagram 195). When using the glass-paper hold the abrasive sheet round a small block of wood as demonstrated in the same diagram.

PAINTING

The outside of the house should be painted with good quality oilbound paints; for the interior either oilbound or waterbound colours can be used. Finely ground poster colours dry quickly and give a smooth and attractive surface.

Before applying any paint, give all the surfaces to be coloured a gentle but thorough rub-down with a very fine grade of glass-paper, called 'flour paper'. When using oilbound colours, make sure that you stir the paint properly; go on stirring for some time after the colour appears to have a uniform consistency.

To achieve best results with oilbound colours, apply at least two coats of undercoating before applying the final top coat. A surface of paint built up in several thin stages looks better than one that has been applied in fewer, thicker coats. Rub each coat lightly with fine glasspaper, when it is dry, before applying the next. The top coat should be laid off with very light brush strokes, finishing each stroke with the tips of the hairs or bristles. This final coat should not be rubbed down.

For picture frames or parts of the fireplace silver, etc. you can use metallic colours which are available in small tins and bottles made specially for model-makers. Sometimes these tins and bottles contain so much fluid that it is difficult to get a satisfactory lustre, however thoroughly the mixture is stirred. You may therefore have to drain some of the liquid away with clean blotting-paper before using the paint.

DECORATING WITH WALLPAPER

Before you paper any of the rooms in the miniature house, you will have to think about what patterns and colours are available to match the colour schemes used in the various parts of the house. There are wallpapers which have been designed specially for miniature houses. The patterns are reduced to a suitable scale so that they do not overpower the miniature furniture, and one sheet of this 'dolls' house' wallpaper, costing only a few pence, will be quite large enough for any of the rooms you have made.

For marking and cutting out the wallpaper use a ruler, pencil, set square and a pair of scissors. Each piece of wallpaper should fit precisely to the corresponding piece of wood, but you can leave some edges ⅛ in. or so oversize if they are to be in a position where you can trim them exactly to size when the adhesive is dry. Try each piece in place as soon as you have cut it out (see diagram 196). For trimming use a steel-backed razor-blade or a sharp pair of scissors.

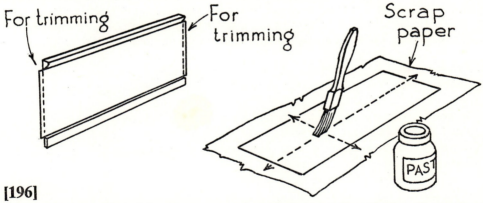

For trimming   For trimming   Scrap paper

[196]

Use any suitable cold-water paste or paperhangers' paste for sticking the paper to the walls. With some adhesives it may be advisable to put a thin coat on the wooden wall surface, as well as on the back of the paper.

To keep adhesive from spoiling the front of the wallpaper, put each piece face downwards on scrap paper and brush the paste from the centre outwards (see diagram 196). The bristles of the brush will then carry the paste safely over the cut edges and will not work it back underneath.

When the pasted paper is put in position on the wall, smooth away any air bubbles with a clean cloth, working again from the centre to the edges of the paper.

SUGGESTIONS FOR DECORATING THE ROOMS

The Sitting-Room: You could decorate this in different tones of gold, like the sitting-room shown in the colour plate facing page 32. The ceiling there has been covered with silver paper, but you could also use a paperbacked metallic paper. Such a colour scheme would give the room a warm and welcoming atmosphere.

The Dining-Room: You could choose strong, exotic colours, for example black and gold. These make an unusual but ideal background for natural wood furniture, as you can see in the colour plate facing page 33. The curtains could be made from material in a rich olive-green.

The Kitchen: As in the kitchen shown in the colour plate facing page 48, you can paint the walls and most of the furniture in pure white, adding a few areas of warm, strong colours—a bright yellow surface for the table, the working surface of the sink, and the floor, vermilion for the top of the washer, and turquoise for the handles on the cupboards, etc.

The Parents' Bedroom: Your colour scheme for this room could be based on pale blue and white (see colour plate facing page 49), using wallpaper with almost the same pattern as in the dining-room, which would give a feeling of continuity in the house. The bedcovers could be made from material in strong, bold colours.

The Children's Bedroom: There the basic colours might be pink, white and scarlet as in the room in the colour plate facing page 64. Candy-striped wallpaper, star-spangled ceiling paper, scarlet carpets and curtains, and creamy-white bedspreads would give this room a gay and bright atmosphere.

The Playroom: For this you could again use strong primary colours like bright red, sunshine yellow and ultramarine blue: see colour plate facing page 48. An effective contrast to these bright colours could be achieved by painting the large surfaces of the walls in white and the floor in black. For the ceiling the same star-studded paper might be used as in the children's bedroom.

The Bathroom: This could be decorated in almost any colour—pink, orange, red, even black, or, like the bathroom shown in the colour plate facing page 65, in diluted blues and greens.

The Hall and Cloakroom: As in the back hall and the cloakroom shown in the colour plate facing page 65, you could paint the walls and the ceilings white, and use pale neutral floorings to achieve an impression of spaciousness. The front hall and the landing could be decorated as those shown in the colour plate facing page 17.

CURTAINS AND OTHER SOFT FURNISHINGS

When you have finished making the various pieces of furniture, add covers and cushions to the beds, settee and armchairs. If you should not want to sew the bedcovers, you can simply cut out strips and pieces of material and fasten them in place with Copydex.

Curtains which appear as if hanging in folds can be made quite easily. Cut pieces of corrugated cardboard (see diagram 197) and fasten them to the pieces of material (centre drawing). Finally add a stripwood pelmet to complete the window.

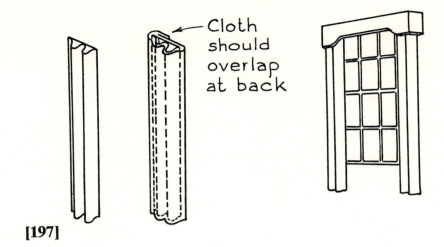

Cloth should overlap at back

[197]

FLOOR COVERINGS

For the floors in the hall and the two reception rooms use paper which represents parquet flooring.

The treads of the staircase as well as the floors of the landing and in the bedrooms should be covered with material that represents soft, luxurious carpet, like suede-textured household papers or very thin felts, sold specially for craftworkers by Messrs. Dryads of Leicester.

The kitchen and bathroom floors and the floor in the children's playroom can be covered with thin Vinyl floor tiles. You can trim these tiles quite easily with a sharp pair of scissors and then fasten them down with Evo-stik or any other suitable adhesive.

LIGHTING

When you look at the finished miniature house you will find that there is ample space left in the attics and under the floors of the lower rooms where you can fit batteries and wires for the lighting equipment.

Diagram 198 shows how three $1\frac{1}{2}$ volt bulbs can be run in series on a $4\frac{1}{2}$ volt battery. When bulbs are connected in series in this way, the sum of their voltage ratings must equal the battery voltage.

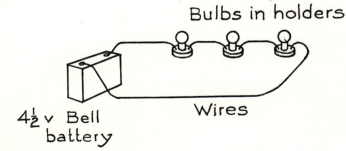

Bulbs in holders

Wires

$4\frac{1}{2}$ v Bell battery

[198]

The following addition sum will explain this:

$$1\frac{1}{2} + 1\frac{1}{2} + 1\frac{1}{2} = 4\frac{1}{2}$$

A 3 volt bulb in series with a $1\frac{1}{2}$ volt bulb ($3 + 1\frac{1}{2} = 4\frac{1}{2}$) would not necessarily work as well, since the voltages of the bulbs are not the same.

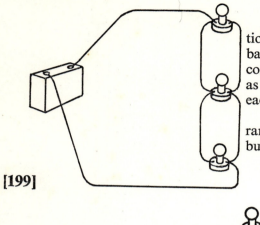

[199]

Diagram 199 gives an example of 'parallel connection'. The bulb holders are wired up in a chain, and the battery is connected across the two sides. In parallel connection each bulb must be rated at the same voltage as the battery. For example, if a 4½ volt battery is used, each of the bulbs must be 4½ volt.

Diagram 200 shows an alternative method of arranging a parallel connection. The same battery and bulbs are used, but each bulb is wired up independently.

[200]

[201]

Switch

When bulbs are arranged in series, all can be governed by a single switch (see diagram 201). In the case of parallel connection any one bulb may be fitted with its own switch, or one switch may be used to govern all the bulbs (see diagram 202). Diagram 203 shows two bulbs, each with its own switch.

One battery may run several circuits, some in parallel, some in series, each with whatever switching it needs. However, if too many bulbs are run off one battery this will be finished in a comparatively short time. You may prefer, therefore, to use a transformer.

When using a 'bell' or similar transformer, connect its main terminals to a power or lighting socket. The output terminals will take the place of the battery. A transformer with an input of 200–250 volt A.C. and an output of 4.5 volt 1.5 amp would be suitable for most miniature houses.

[202]

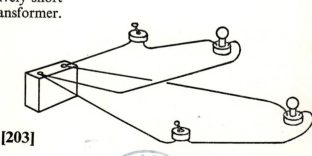

[203]

96